Praise for *Holding On While Letting Go*

"*Holding On While Letting Go* is prec
to instill confidence, mental health
dren, while building a connected a
at all ages. Carl's Four Freedoms show how to
healthy, well-adjusted adults. The book is a resource to help parents
adapt, encourage, and grow themselves help—so ultimately we are
all at our best."

—**Elizabeth Hamilton-Guarino,** mom of four sons
and author of *The Change Guidebook*

Holding On
WHILE
Letting Go

Holding On
WHILE
Letting Go

Parenting Your Child
Through the Four Freedoms
of Adolescence

Carl Pickhardt, PhD
author of *Who Stole My Child?*

Health Communications, Inc.
Boca Raton, Florida

www.hcibooks.com

Library of Congress Cataloging-in-Publication Data
is available through the Library of Congress

© 2022 Carl Pickhardt, Ph.D.

ISBN-13: 978-07573-2423-9 (Paperback)
ISBN-10: 07573-2423-1 (Paperback)
ISBN-13: 978-07573-2424-6 (ePub)
ISBN-10: 07573-2424-X (ePub)

Publisher: Health Communications, Inc.
        301 Crawford Blvd., Suite 200
        Boca Raton, FL 33432-1653

Cover, interior design and formatting by Larissa Hise Henoch

Disclaimer

• • •

I am an applied psychologist, not an academic one. I write from observational experience and reflection, not from experimentation or literature review. I created the ideas in this book to capture some of the complexity of the changing parent/teenager relationship as, in retirement from private practice, I reflect back on my experience giving counseling and parenting talks over many years. This said, all of the examples used and quotes given are fictitious, constructed to illustrate psychological points. •

Dedication

• • •

Once upon a time there lived a girl or boy who felt ready for a change. They didn't want to be defined and treated as just a little child anymore. Restless and dissatisfied, more frequently distracted and bored, the young person now wanted something very important—more *freedom to grow*. But how?

Looking forward, they dimly saw a pathway open before them that left childhood behind and led to an older future far ahead. And while they were excited by the possibilities, they also felt scared of the unknown. So they must be brave.

Then a troubling change began to happen at home. As they pushed against and pulled away and got around their parents for more running room, these ruling adults, who used to be mostly happy and pleased, now acted more frequently concerned and irritated, less fun and understanding to be around. Why so?

The answer is that the harder half of growing up called "adolescence" was coming last, making it also the harder half of parenting. The child's ten- to twelve-year coming-of-age passage was beginning—the adventurous and abrasive process of separation that would finally transform the girl or boy into a functionally independent and fittingly individual young woman or young man at journey's end.

In response, parents would struggle to practice the art of *holding on while letting go,* insisting where they must and allowing where they could, and in the process undergoing transformation too. In fits and starts, they would gradually relinquish leadership control as the young person assumed more self-management authority.

So this book is dedicated to the loyal parents and determined teenagers who strive to stay caringly and communicatively connected as *four adolescent drives for freedom* gradually grow them apart, which they are meant to do.

Contents

● ● ●

Introduction

· · ·

Get Ready, Get Set, Go!

"When you choose to have a child,
you have agreed to have an adolescent."

Surely, if one word is commonly associated with the image of the teenager it is *freedom*. The very breath of adolescent life, freedom is the power to make one's own decisions, to find one's path, to not be told how to act, to become different, to oppose social restraint, to explore the world outside of family, to test and contest limits, to dare the untried, to follow one's dream, to run with friends, to act more grown up, to determine one's direction. Freedom: you can't grow up without it!

To cope with this irresistible call, I believe it's best for parents to be prepared for changes to come. To this end, this book explores how *four basic freedoms* can sequentially and cumulatively drive the period of growing up commonly termed "adolescence." Each freedom is linked to what I see as one of four successive "stages" of development that begin with separating from childhood at the outset and winding down ten to twelve years later with the departure into self-managed independence at the end.

Of course, these stages are only approximations. Not every parent will experience each freedom issue exactly the same way with every teenager since the adolescent passage is subject to great individual variation.

However, I believe these four unfolding and accumulating freedoms that constitute the major sections of this book generally apply:

1. **Freedom from rejection of childhood** to stop acting as just a child (around the late elementary school years).

2. **Freedom with association with peers** to form a second family of friends (around the middle school years).

3. **Freedom for advanced experimentation** to signify becoming more adult (around the high school years).

4. **Freedom to claim emancipation** to become one's ruling authority (around the college-age years).

The four larger sections of this book describe some specific adolescent and parenting challenges commonly associated with each freedom.

Introductory to these sections are four chapters that prepare the reader's way. These chapters address

• adolescence as change;
• holding on while letting go;
• communicating when growing apart;
• the importance of heeding freedom's call.

I have written conversationally, as my goal in this book is to talk with parents about how four sequential freedoms energize teenage development. I believe that the less surprised parents are by common adolescent changes, the more appropriate and effective their responses are likely to be. If they can keep their expectations ahead of the young person's growth curve, when the next step is taken, they can respond with more power of understanding and less risk of overreaction: "I didn't want her to try this in high school, but I thought there was a chance she might, so at least I'm not completely surprised."

Over many years of writing columns, blogs, and books of adult nonfiction and young adult fiction, I have told and retold the coming-of-age story that continues to endlessly fascinate me. Before retiring from private practice, for over thirty years I was engaged in counseling and giving public talks about the parent/adolescent relationship.

With this much experience, you might think that I would have arrived at a clear picture of what is going on during the child's adolescence, but this is not the case. The more I've observed and pondered, the more complicated this life transition has become for me to understand. It's been like trying to assemble a puzzle of infinite pieces, never getting the larger picture exactly right.

Thus, the best I can offer parents is an *approximation*. This book is a *tool kit of ideas*, an estimate of tendencies, some ways to think about what is happening, why it is happening, and how parents might want to respond—it is not a statement of certainties.

Does this small catalogue of common adolescent changes and challenges mean that all parents are destined for some kind of agony when their daughter or son enters the teenage years? *No, absolutely not.* Although the four drives for youthful freedom yield often-surprising events, in the great majority of cases I believe a child's adolescence does not significantly derail the young person or disrupt family life.

However, growth will occur, youthful change will happen, parenting issues will arise, and adjustments must usually be made. Not only is an adolescent no longer a child, but now she or he has become an adult-in-training. Readiness for more capacity and responsibility must be practiced, and I believe the parents' job is to support this preparation.

Along the way, parents don't always make the right call, and the young person doesn't always make the wise decision. Good children and good parents sometimes make poor choices in the normal trial-and-error process of the young person's growing up. A "bad" choice doesn't mean the child or the parenting is bad, only that both are human. From this hit-and-miss experience, each learns a lot from what happens as they grow.

I can declare this point with confidence. Since no two teenagers and no two parents are exactly alike, and since every family situation is unique, no one parenting approach works for all. Thus, reading my ideas, feel free to take what you like, discount what you do not, and use what helps you to keep carrying on. *Figuring out your own parenting way* during the adolescent passage with each individual child is what I hope this book may enable you to do.

Chapter One

Adolescence Is Change

● ● ●

"I'm not the same as I was."

A way to think about adolescence is simply as one example of *life change*—that evolving process of alteration that continually keeps upsetting and resetting the terms of everyone's existence all their lives, creating both loss and opportunity as people grow. Within us, between us, and outside of us, welcome and unwelcome, nothing remains exactly the same for very long. Partly chosen but often not, in one form or another change plays a leading role in how each person's destiny unfolds.

Change takes some getting used to—relinquishing the old and engaging with the new—everyone redefining themselves in the process to some degree: "He's not the little child he used to be. He says we're not the same parents either, and maybe so." Thus, in a relationship, change in one party can beget change in the other. And while much that happens may be planned and anticipated, much also comes as a surprise: "I never thought this would happen!" Because much of adolescence is emergent and unanticipated, it's best for parents to be informed where they can and ready for the unexpected where they cannot.

Estrangement

To some degree, adolescent change will be estranging in the family. As the teenager becomes more fascinated with current fads and fashions, the less current parents can become—leading to being more out of touch in their own and in youthful eyes. Thus a cultural distance develops between the up-to-date adolescent who is expert on what momentarily matters, who is "with it," and the outdated parent mired in what used to be who is sometimes accused, and sometimes feels, "out of it." The fashions, norms, and icons that shaped the parents' growing up are not the same as those that shape their teenager now. This contributes to the cultural generation gap that is separating them and the young person: "We're behind the times that he's fascinated by. We have to scramble to keep up!"

What Is Change?

Operationally, change is in evidence when some condition or circumstance *stops* or *starts* or *increases* or *decreases,* thereby disrupting the fixed, repetitive, familiar, stable, normal, routine, or established conduct of our lives.

Any major life change usually turns out to be some compound of these four kinds of change. For example, with *adolescent change* the growing girl or boy must *stop* acting childlike, must *start* acting older, must *increase* worldly experience, and must *decrease* dependence on parents.

No wonder managing increasing change can feel more complicated and demanding as one proceeds through the coming-of-age passage. Now the young person can never return home to that simpler, sheltered, and more secure beginning of their lives, sometimes missing what must be left behind. And parents can fondly recall that old, golden time too: "We had such simple, sweet times together!" Change can make life interesting and fulfilling but also chaotic and painful. However, coping with change—this mix of gain and loss—is what the parent and adolescent must learn to do.

Dancing with Adolescent Changes

Change creates what is new and different, unfamiliar and unknown, so for parents, the child becoming an adolescent can take some adjustment. No news there: so what's the problem? Simply this: while shared similarities in relationships can make it easier to find comfortable common ground, human differences can make it harder for people to get along. For example, consider the contrast between parenting a child and parenting an adolescent.

Childhood is often ruled by similarity to parents because the child wants to be like them (imitation) and do what the parents want (compliance) to create a strong attachment, this bond creating security and a trusted connection upon which children can depend.

Adolescence is often ruled by contrast to childhood and parents because the young person is now differentiating for more expressive *individuality* (diversity) and detaching for more social *independence* (autonomy), with increasing separation and redefinition accomplished on both counts.

Growth Creates Change

Come adolescence, the young person is now undergoing change on four levels of personal redefinition.

- **Characteristics** are changing, like developing sexual maturity.
- **Values** are changing, like identifying with a culture of peers.
- **Habits** are changing, like becoming increasingly nocturnal.
- **Wants** are changing, like wanting more personal freedom.

When the parent in counseling declares, "This is not the child I've always known," they are not misperceiving.

From here on, parents must learn to dance with more differences with their daughter or son than before, practicing *four steps* with which they may not have much experience: *accepting, respecting, tolerating,* and *negotiating.* "Dancing" means taking these steps to accommodate growing differences between parent and child, working through those differences they can, and working around those they cannot as adolescence gradually moves them apart.

Change Creates Differences

As the child changes into an adolescent, a lot of parental adjustment to growing differences is required. For example, contrasting *characteristics,* discordant values, incompatible habits, and conflicting wants are all individual differences that can make it more difficult for parent and adolescent to get along sometimes. Take these differences one at a time.

- **Characteristic differences** are inherent, unchosen, vested aspects of oneself that basically define how a person is—their sex, physical makeup, temperament, and personality, for example. Characteristics cannot be changed. In relationships, they must be *accepted*. One characteristic of an adolescent is that now she or he is becoming more womanly or manly in role and appearance. To say to the adolescent, "Wearing clothes that draw attention to your developing body is not okay; you need to keep dressing like you always have," discourages or disapproves how the girl or boy is physically growing.

- **Value differences** are deeply vested beliefs that are so powerfully held that when a person runs out of reasons to defend them, they are still in place—like about right or wrong, valuable or worthless, meaningful or pointless, for example. Values are deeply set. In relationships, such differences must be *respected*. One teenage value is identifying with the culture of one's peers, like current entertainment and popular icons who define their generation. To say to the adolescent, "I don't care what 'everyone' likes; you're not listening to that kind of music in this home!" can be prejudicial against youthful tastes.

- **Habit differences** are practiced patterns of behavior that with repetition become more automatic than intentional—like how one is routinely orderly or disorderly, prompt or late, speaks up or shuts up, for example. Habits can be intractable. In relationships they must often be *tolerated*. One habit of adolescence is increasingly challenging parental authority, arguing more to contest disagreement. To say to the adolescent, "Don't you ever talk back to me!" refuses to discuss what the adolescent questions and shuts speaking up and communication down.

- **Want differences** express what one would like to happen or not happen that motivate much daily behavior—like desires, interests, and goals, for example. Wants are subject to changing inclinations and circumstances. In relationships they can be *negotiated*. One common want of an adolescent is having more independence to create more room to grow. To say to the adolescent, "I'll decide when you're ready to try that, not you!" forecloses on discussing preparedness for undertaking behavior appropriate to someone older. So now there may be more bargaining: "For us to allow you this freedom, this is what we need from you first."

What to remember is that the first three levels of differences—*characteristics, values,* and *habits* are firmly fixed and, if not impossible, at least very hard to change, while *wants* have more flexibility. So, use this distinction to your advantage.

Managing Disagreement

Neither parent nor adolescent should be in the business of altering the other person's characteristics, values, or habits since by doing so each person is faulted for what they cannot change. The relationship can suffer by one party becoming dissatisfied and impatient and the other party becoming offended and injured.

What works best is for the concerned parent and adolescent to translate differences that can't be changed (characteristics, values, habits) into what may be changed (wants), which can then be worked out with concession or compromise.

Characteristics: "Now that your body is growing up, let's talk about ways we both *want* you to be able to dress older and express yourself." These differences need to be *accepted*.

Values: "Now that you live in a new community of peers, let's talk about ways we both *want* you to be able to fit in and keep up with those things that matter to you." These differences need to be *respected*.

Habits: "Now that you increasingly question our limits and directions, let's talk about ways we both *want* to turn disagreements into
discussions to create more communication between us." These differences need to be *tolerated*.

Wants: "Now that you desire more room for new freedom, let's
talk about the risks involved and work out ways we both *want* for you
to safely grow." These differences need to be *negotiated*.

In these discussions, parents can express sincere belief: "The differences that increasingly contrast us can also connect us when we
can talk about them and listen to what each other has to say." It's a
challenging dance parents have to do with their adolescent—accepting, respecting, tolerating, or negotiating growing differences between
them, all the while using differences to generate discussion to create
communication that connects them as they increasingly grow apart.

The parental mantra for dancing with adolescent change is this:
*"We will be firm where we have to; we will be flexible where we can;
we will explain our needs and reasons; and we always want to listen
to whatever you have to say, so long as it is spoken in a respectful and
unharmful way."*

Chapter Two

Holding On While Letting Go

● ● ●

"Just do it for me and let me decide!"

From an adolescent's perspective, parenting can seem simple: "Just give me what I need and let me do what I want." However, for the parent it's more complicated than that. Parents must wrestle with an ongoing problem of judgment with the still dependent but more freedom-driven adolescent. The challenging parental question often is *when and how much to hold on and restrain by saying "no"* and *when and how much to start letting go and release by saying "yes."*

As the young person pushes for more self-determination ("I can handle it!"), parents have to weigh the risks ("What is the possibility of hurt?"). When it comes to gatekeeping adolescent freedom, saying no or saying yes can be very problematic decisions that parents often have to make. Consider some of this complexity.

13

To begin, parents often find themselves caught in a *common child-raising conflict*: how much to control and *hold on* by saying no and how much to allow and *let go* by saying yes. When to prohibit and when to permit? Parents may often decide on a mix of protective and permissive decisions by insisting on some conditions first: *holding on while letting go.* "You can do it on your own, but you need to check in with us while you do." So, for the sake of parental comfort, the new driver calls in after arriving at her destination and again when leaving to come home. Parents explain, "As you demonstrate more capability, we'll trust you more on your own."

Holding On–Letting Go Conflicts

Freedom that is exciting for the teenager can feel alarming for the parents who ask themselves two kinds of questions.

- **Holding-on questions** about control can be "Should we delay?" "Should we caution?" "Should we prepare?" Think of learning to drive a car.
- **Letting-go questions** about freedom can be "Should we encourage?" "Should we trust?" "Should we risk?" Think of starting to date.

After the young person has claimed functional independence, usually around the college-age years, these are no longer material questions, but until then, they definitely are. And it can be really hard to get the mix of holding on and letting go, of saying no or yes, exactly right. Hold on too tight and risk preventing education through over-protection. Charges the teenager, "You never let me do anything!" Let go too much and risk endangering through neglect. Charges the teenager, "You left too much up to me!" The result is that parents often choose to operate more contractually, mixing some holding on with some letting go: "We'll give some of what you want if you give us some of we want first."

Common Conflicts

Always about freedom, common hold-on-or-let-go conflicts can sound like this: "Should I notice or ignore, withhold or give, suspect or trust, be firm or be flexible, insist or relent, pursue or give up, be strict or be lax, speak up or shut up, correct or tolerate, remind or not, push or back off, disagree or agree, question or accept, encounter or avoid, disallow or permit?" These judgment calls increase the perplexity of parenting an adolescent.

Each case presents different consequences depending on which way parents choose. And reversal is okay. Based on new evidence or simple reconsideration, parents may change their minds, holding on instead of letting go: "I thought you were ready for this, but I was wrong." Or they may let go instead of holding on: "You're more responsible now than I gave you credit for."

From Holding On to Letting Go

For sure, parenting an adolescent can feel different than parenting a child. While the child was content to operate mostly within the family circle, within parental oversight, and accept the parental no, the adolescent now becomes restless for more social running room and complains about the parental worry and restraint. Now she or he wants to be out in the larger world in the company of eager, like-minded peers who have exciting ideas. And now freedom that a young person might reject when operating alone becomes harder to resist when adventurous friends are encouraging and urging them on: "Everyone else wanted to give it a try, so I did too." The company of friends can affect the power of personal choice.

Wanting closeness and control, parents *held on* to the child to secure basic trust and dependency. They all felt safer this way. Saying no felt protective. Come adolescence, however, parents do more *letting go* to foster more experience. "Yes" feels more liberating. However, by supporting growing separation, parents pay a price: they encourage risk-taking, endure more uncertainty, and suffer more worry in the process. Letting go can be a stressful part of parenting: "I don't want her to get harmed!" Parenting an adolescent can be more anxiety provoking than parenting a child.

For all concerned, letting go can be scary. Adolescent letting go is often an act of courage for the changing child: "I hope I'm not sorry!" The same goes for the parents: "We hope we're right!" There are always risks to letting go and to saying yes—for parents and adolescents. "Is he, and are we, ready for him to hang out at the mall with his teenage friends?" "Is she, and are we, ready for her to go to a college party?" And when misfortune strikes, parents can fault themselves: "We shouldn't have let it happen!"

Self-blame is usually not helpful. Reestimating adolescent readiness is what is needed. "There are some things you still need to learn and practice. So let's get started." Even after providing preparation, when granting freedom, parents are always taking chances with the welfare of their child. Letting go can thus be part of the agony of parenting—putting the beloved at risk for the sake of growing up. Fortunately, as the teenager gets more accustomed to risk-taking, showing more evidence of responsibility when they do, parents grow more comfortable with allowing increased power of choice. Moreover, the ill effects of excess freedom can be informative: "I'll never try that again!"

Adolescence Demands Adjustment

As suggested earlier, adolescence proceeds along two major avenues of development. There is *detachment* for independence to grow as more *separation* from childhood and parents are created. And there is differentiation for individuality to grow as more *contrast* to childhood and parents is expressed. In both cases increased freedom is required. Parents who have little patience with the first and low tolerance for the second can have a hard time with this adjustment.

The question is how to encompass these changes. Parents don't just stop holding on and start letting go; they combine both. The parenting challenge is complicated. *As parents back off and respect the growing separation and do more letting go, they must also continue to provide some ongoing oversight and preparation by holding on.* The mix can be challenging to get right. "We want him to be responsible for doing his homework, but we intend to check enough to see that it is all getting adequately accomplished."

Adolescent Estrangement

To some degree, the transition from parenting a child and mostly holding on to parenting an adolescent and doing more letting go can feel *estranging*—like going from being an insider to more of an outsider in your young person's life: "I was told a lot when she was a child, but now that she is older, I'm told less;" "I was primary company, and now peers come first;" "We used to share enjoyments, but now there's less that we like to do together."

For most parents, experiencing estrangement with their teenager feels only occasional: "I don't understand how he can enjoy playing that video game!" For some it can be more often: "She's too busy with friends to spend time with me!" *The challenge for parents is not to let healthy separation become unhealthy estrangement where the parent feels cut off and the adolescent feels abandoned.* Parents must still hold on while letting go. They must forgo some control to allow growth, while maintaining enough active communication to stay in adequate contact—permitting more freedom while keeping in adequate touch.

How Parents Experience Estrangement

Letting go to allow more freedom can engender expressions of parental estrangement that can sound like this:

"I've lost my best buddy."

"I don't know her as well."

"We have less in common."

"We live in separate worlds."

"He wants less time with me."

"It's harder to stay connected."

"We see things differently."

"I don't matter as much."

"I'm less informed about what's going on."

"It's harder to get time together now."

"She's more private."

Such parental expressions of estrangement announce an adjustment to how adolescence grows parent and child apart, which it is meant to do. No love is necessarily lost, but more separation does occur. Offline and online preoccupations—youthful entertainments, adventures, fashions, fads, ideals, activities, preferences, priorities, and peer relationships—all combine to create a competing world of primary experience apart from family where the increasingly self-absorbed and socially active teenager desires to spend more time and where parents do not.

Engagement and Not Estrangement

The question for the parent, then, is how to stay communicatively and caringly connected to their teenager as their worlds increasingly diverge. How to hold on while doing more letting go? This change need not be alienating. How can they stay constructively engaged? Consider a few holding-on strategies while they are doing more letting go.

Bridge differences with interest. "Can you help me appreciate what you enjoy doing now? I'd love to better understand." The teenager is treated as a teacher.

Inconvenient listening. "Whenever you feel like talking, I want to stop what I'm doing and hear whatever you have to say." Teenage communication is treated as a priority.

Social welcoming. "I really enjoy meeting your friends when they come over." Teenage companions are valued at home.

Household work. "Everyone pitching in with help shows how all of us support the family." The teenager is treated as a contributor.

Invitations for play. "I'm always open to doing together what would be fun for us." The teenager is treated as a companion.

Offering assistance. "Always know that when problems arise, I will be there to help if you wish." The teenager is treated as entitled to parental support.

Cheering on. "Way to go! I'm so impressed by how you're doing." The teenager is treated as worth encouraging.

Personal sharing. "I want to tell you about what is happening with me." The teenager is treated as a confidante.

Parents understand the more complicated adolescent less well than the comparatively simple child. This is not a problem to stop but a growing reality to accept. Growing up, growing older, and growing old always lead toward more complexity. Knowing their teenager less does not mean loving or valuing them less, only that more independence and individuality are growing between them. Because the adolescent is often more self-preoccupied by growing challenges and complexity, parents must take the initiative and lead the effort for them to stay in adequate family touch.

Parents as Gatekeepers

Holding on while letting go, parents are gatekeepers—regulating much adolescent freedom with prohibition, preparation, and permission. Every time, parents are making judgment calls. In the process, parenting can feel like a presumptuous occupation. After all, who really knows for sure how this job is supposed to be accomplished?

Self-appointed "experts" may be helpful but are not the final answer. The most they can do is be thought-provoking. At the last, *every parent with every child and adolescent has to create their own best practices.* This is the loneliness of parenting, which is why having a partner, family, friends, or helper to confide in and consult with is so important. Social isolation does a parent no favors, creating insecurity from feeling alone and risking distortion from losing perspective. Bottom line: *for adequate support, have some trusted adult company to keep.*

Raising the Stakes

Adolescence raises the childhood stakes of personal freedom as more worldly exposure, outside company, and functioning as an older person are sought. "It's the contrast between learning to ride a bike and to drive a car" was how one parent explained this quantum differ-ence. "There's much more to worry about now." Parents still hold on to what they want, but they have to let go and deal with more that is unexpected, contested, and compromised. How to handle what feels like a lot more responsibility?

Parenting with humility can help, with an absence of arrogance that too much prizes one's rightness and wisdom. Humility accepts: "I don't know all the answers;" "I don't control all that happens;" "I don't always make the right decision." In reality, *parenting an adolescent is often like the shortsighted leading the blind.* The parent is informed and biased by limited life experience, while the teenager has never grown in this way. So it's a trial-and-error path they must tread together, trusting in this evolving education. During perplexing times, it is no shame for parents to sometimes seek outside social, counseling, or coaching help. It is often the better part of wisdom.

Humility also means moderating ambition, not depending too much on the child's performance: "My teenager should make me look good!" This way is the danger of *vanity parenting*—pushing the teen-ager to achieve so that parents and their parenting look well socially. Here, that statement of congratulations, "I'm proud of you," can be laden with self-serving pressure when it means, "I depend on you to make me proud of me." As the parent feeds off the child's accomplish-ments, the child can feel obligated to support parental self-esteem: "I mustn't disappoint or let them down!"

When congratulating, it's probably best for parents to keep the credit where it belongs and simply say, "Good for you!" Hold on to the power of parental approval, but let go of taking personal credit for the teenager's performance. Now the teenager can freely say, "My parents are happy *for* me, not *because of* me."

The Mixed Responsibility

Responsible parents hold on by maintaining a family structure of healthy rules and expectations in which the young person can safely operate. At the same time, they let go objection to resistance when the teenager inevitably protests: "Why can't I?" "Why must I?" "Why now?" "Tell me why!" Questions of parental authority are not disrespectful. They testify to belief in parental influence. Ignoring what parents say shows disrespect, paying it no mind. So welcome argument and questions. Engage with objections by listening and explaining, and help create a discussion that is also about connecting: "Talking about this, we understand each other better now."

Parental letting go can also be unpopular with their adolescent when freedom feels unwanted. Thus parents let go by allowing and assigning more freedom of operation to be responsible for, about which the teenager might sometimes complain, "Why must it be up to me?" It felt easier to request money as needed and wanted from parents than to live on a fixed monthly personal expense budget now in high school. Total freedom can feel too much to handle: "Too much is left up to me!" Parental rules and restraints can be protective: "I don't like having a curfew, but it does give me an excuse for leaving to go home."

Now there is also more tension to contend with, occasions when parents need to say and mean, "Parenting is not a popularity contest because sometimes we must take a stand for your best interests by holding on to opposition against what you want, and you will not thank us for not letting go." Of course, a teen can criticize the parent for erring in each direction. Accusing the parent of holding on too much, the young person may complain, "You never let me do anything!" Accusing the parent of letting go too much, the young person may complain, "You leave too much up to me!" *Blessed is the parent who can be criticized on both counts.*

At worst, there is the need for parental holding on when the young person acts against their better interest and insists on being let go only to become caught in some cycle of self-defeat. Now parents have some holding on to do.

Cycles of Self-Defeat

The opportunities for self-defeating behavior in adolescence are legion, and it's easy for a young person to sometimes get stuck. *Do not let these patterns of self-defeat go.* Holding on can be trying to help or getting outside help to stop the harm. To illustrate the kinds of holding-on behaviors I mean, consider this partial list to appreciate how varied these self-entrapments can be.

> **Rebellion:** "I won't do whatever I'm told to do."
> **Conformity:** "I'll go along and do whatever to belong."
> **Escape:** "I'll play online to avoid offline work."
> **Procrastination:** "I'll delay and let demands pile up."
> **Dishonesty:** "I'll lie, though it betrays the trust of others."
> **Cheating:** "I'll keep pretending to know more than I really do."
> **Craving:** "I do what's bad for me because it feels good to me."
> **Depression:** "The sadder I get, the less I try to feel better."
> **Anxiety:** "The more scared I feel, the more fearful I act."
> **Helplessness:** "Feeling there's nothing I can do, I just stop trying."

In each case, the young person has become complicit in their own unhappiness by letting it worsen. This complicity will continue unless and until the teenager takes steps—by themselves, with parents, or with outside help—to assume multiple responsibilities. Sometimes in counseling, teenagers take the following steps:

- Confronting harm they are doing to themselves
- Identifying the motivations for acting this way
- Determining the personal costs
- Deciding to correct the error of their ways
- Coming up with a positive action plan
- Putting this constructive alternative into consistent practice.
- Recognizing good efforts being made and better outcomes achieved
- Being patient with not immediately or entirely self-correcting right away

The good thing about complicity in self-defeat is that it retains some power of corrective choice. The twelve-year-old who has been socially uprooted by parental divorce and starting a new school goes on an angry strike against her two single parents: "I'll show you! I'll do the work, but I won't like any of my teachers, I won't make any friends, I won't join any activities, and I'll be really unhappy!" Rebelling against her own self-interest to protest the family split, she is bent on punishing her parents by punishing herself.

With compassion, her parents close ranks and declare, "This is your hurt and angry choice, and we respect that. It is up to you." Then they make a holding-on offer, "But should you ever change your mind and want to make your new school a fun school, please know that we are here to help you do that. In the meantime, we will listen to any unhappiness you want to share."

Cost of Self-Defeat

One of the great costs of protracted self-defeating behavior can be a lowering of self-esteem: "I hate the way I keep doing this to myself!" It's easy for self-defeating behavior to lead to self-blame, beating oneself up for continuing a practice that does more harm than good: "I just keep making things worse!" At that point, self-blame can become another act of self-defeat because it has no encouraging constructive alternative to offer. So parents explain, "Punishing yourself won't help you feel or act any better."

Parents need to pay attention when their teenager appears to be engaged in significant self-defeating behavior because it can injure adolescent growth and lower self-esteem, and in the extreme it can be self-endangering. If parents see it, they need to talk about it—not with criticism, but with concern: "We think you may be hurting yourself by how you're acting, and we'd like to describe what we see." If the young person feels or appears stuck, consider getting some counseling help, because, left unattended, self-defeating behavior can do a lot of harm. This is responsible holding on for parents.

When Parents Are Complicit

Of course, parents can be complicit in keeping the young person from learning from unhappy experience, letting life lessons go, usually wanting to do so to spare their teenager (and perhaps themselves) from further suffering: "We can't bear to see him hurting himself!" To that end they can rationalize, excuse, give multiple second chances, accept more promises, make exceptions, or otherwise rescue the adolescent from unhappy consequences, doing all these things in the name of "helping," which can actually hurt by enabling harmful choices to continue: "We can't bear to see him suffer when he's so sorry for what he did." So forgiveness was given, but it was treated as permission. "I'm sorry," says the penitent teenager. "That's okay," console the parents. Thinks the teenager, *If it's okay, then I can keep doing it again.*

The risk is that by not holding the young person responsible, parents may prevent the young person from vital benefits the choice—consequence connection has to teach: *accountability* and *education.* Now she or he will continue with and possibly worsen immature or unwise decisions, as with the last-stage overspending adolescent: "To keep charging your way out of debt only increases what you owe, and our bailing you out only gets in the way of paying what you owe and learning to live within your means."

Parental holding on sometimes means being willing to hold the adolescent accountable for her or his actions.

Holding On + Letting Go = Accommodation

Come adolescence, parents must learn to dance with many teenage changes. *Accommodation* is how this awkward dance is done.

Accommodation is a two-step parental dance with adolescent change: *adjusting* to what parents cannot alter (letting go) and *insisting* on what they may be able to influence (holding on). Accommodation is a compromise in this way.

Parenting a teenager becomes a series of complicated judgment calls. So, when their sixth-grader adopts a new look that contrasts with what was worn in the elementary grades, one that is unfamiliar or seems inappropriate in parental eyes, parents are told, "This is what everyone wears; I won't fit in if I don't dress like them!" Their daughter or son wants to keep up with the older manner of clothing to suit the fashion of middle school.

So comes this parental *accommodation*: "We understand your need to dress differently now, but we want to discuss how and to what degree."

Parental accommodations to common adolescent changes come in so many forms, a few examples of which follow.

- Parents adjust to *less communication* but insist on honesty: "We know you won't confide as much, but we still expect to be adequately and accurately informed."
- Parents adjust to *more disorganization* but insist on adequate order: "We know keeping track of your belongings is harder now, but we expect regular effort to do so."
- Parents adjust to *more forgetfulness* but insist on honoring commitments: "We know remembering everything is challenging now, but we expect you to keep agreements with us."
- Parents adjust to *less control* but insist on core compliance. "We know you want to follow your own rules, but we also expect you to abide by the basics of ours."
- Parents adjust to *more push for freedom* but insist on responsibility: "We support you making more choices, but we expect you to own and face the natural consequences of doing so."
- Parents adjust to adolescents' *worldly curiosity* but insist on giving what cautionary information they can: "When you decide to try what we wish you wouldn't yet, we want to talk about protections and precautions to take."
- Parents adjust to the growing *importance of friends* but insist on family membership: "We know social life matters more now, but we expect adequate participation at home as well."

- Parents adjust to *increased peer pressure* but insist that independent choice prevails: "We know it's hard to resist going along, but we expect you to do what you know is right."
- Parents adjust to *more requests for money* but insist on budgeting to meet expenses: "We know there's more you want, but you must manage what we give to make it last."
- Parents adjust to *more delay* but insist on completion: "We know it feels easy to put off what you're asked to do, but we will pursue our requests until they are met."
- Parents adjust to *more resistance to homework* but insist it is accomplished: "We know sometimes you want to skip assignments, but we will supervise to see you get them done."
- Parents adjust to *internet preoccupation* but insist on adequate screen-free time: "We know online activity is of value, but we want you to have sufficient offline activity too."
- Parents adjust to *nighttime freedom* but insist what bedtime and staying-out time is going to be: "We know you want to stay up and out longer, but we want a curfew to establish how late this will be."
- Parents adjust to *more intensity* but insist on talking and not acting it out: "We know this is a more emotional time, but we expect you to tell us, rather than show us, when you're feeling upset."
- Parents adjust to *more arguing* but insist on firmness they must take: "While we want to hear all you have to say, sometimes our decision may remain unchanged."
- Parents adjust to *more risk-taking* but insist on predictive preparation: "As you take more chances, we expect you to think ahead and prepare for possible problems and dangers."

- Parents adjust to *more disagreements* but insist they are conducted safely: "Conflict is natural but never an excuse for either of us to act harmfully or say hurtful words."

Accommodation is not about parents always getting their way with the adolescent because they won't. However, if they mix *letting go and adjusting where they must* with *holding on and insisting where they can*, some consent with what they want, and some freedom the teenager wants will result. And as their teenager grows older, on each side "some" is going to have to be enough.

Nagging as Parental Holding On

Of all the forms of parental holding on, nagging may be the most burdensome on all concerned. As an adolescent once described it to me, "I cannot fathom the mental processes that lead to nagging. It is counterproductive in relation to getting the actual task done and builds resentment on both sides. The nagger is in a persistent state of victimhood, the nagged because they are continually harassed."

Despite agreeing with much of what he described, I believe parental nagging can still be honorable work, sometimes even constructively done. By my definition, *parental nagging is the use of repeated reminding to convince a reluctant child to abide a family rule or to cooperate with an adult request.*

When excessively applied, nagging can feel unrewarding and taxing on the giving and receiving ends. As the teenager above suggests, it can wear on both sides of the relationship.

- **For the nagged:** Constant nagging is aggressive, invasive, and oppressive, "I hate it when you keep on nagging me!"
- **For the nagger:** Constant nagging is demanding, irritating, and exhausting, "I hate having to keep nagging you!"

If both parties find this behavior so agonizing, why is this unpopular act of holding on so frequently done?

Why Nag?

Partly, I believe, adolescent change is the culprit. For the young person, growing independence fuels the desire to operate more on one's own terms, in the process becoming increasingly intolerant of being told what to do. So now there can be more active resistance to authority in the form of *arguing* and more passive resistance in the form of *delay*, this last is where parental nagging can be employed. Why?

- Nagging shows the parent is serious: "I repeat to show that what I want is important to me."
- Nagging keeps track of what needs to be done: "I keep reminding so you don't forget what is important for you."
- Nagging is an act of parental follow-through: "I keep after you until the task is accomplished."

The Conflict

At issue for the more independent-minded teenager can be pushing for a compromise: "You can tell me what, I'll tell you when, and when I get enough 'when' I'll do what you want—at least partly." Delay shows that adult authority has no power of command until and unless the teenager agrees to give consent. Conflict can ensue.

- Adolescent delay can express independence: "Whether I do what you want when you want is up to me!" ("If I delay long enough, maybe you'll let it go.")
- Parental nagging can express willingness to follow through: "We'll back up our words with supervision." ("If we hold on to

what we want with enough persistence, maybe you'll finally do what we want.")

Since nagging can be irritating to receive and give, it's best for parents to use it selectively, keep it specifically directed, and communicate it matter-of-factly (unemotionally): "I am asking you again to please wash and put away the dirty dishes left on the kitchen table after your snack."

To be fair, adolescents can do their share of nagging too, as parents of a willful teenager sometimes testify, "When we say 'no,' why can't you just accept that? Instead you keep hounding us to change our minds. You keep asking and asking and asking for us to finally give in!" Now, who is nagging whom? Neither party would resort to nagging if it was not sometimes successful. This act of determined holding on can be effective.

Differentiating Nagging

Consider these three levels of parental nagging. The first two are often serviceable by providing oversight; the third is often stressful by becoming oppressive.

> **Informative nagging** can be reminding: "Remember what needs doing."
>
> **Confirming nagging** can be checking: "Did you manage to get it done?"
>
> **Insistent nagging** can be pursuit: "I'll keep after you until you do it!"

Parents should generally confine most nagging to the first two levels, which are most lightly given and received. It is best not to rely on insistent nagging too much because that is what youthful objection (quoted earlier) finds hardest to bear.

An Alternative

If the wear and tear of parental nagging as pursuit is dragging down all parties, a less objectionable but effective alternative for this holding on is *working the exchange points.*

The adolescent is still dependent on parents for all manner of permissions and provisions that the parent is usually glad to give because that is part of their job. However, the relationship needs to be a two-way street, an exchange with each party cooperating and contributing for both to get along.

So, instead of oppressively nagging to get what was promised but has not been forthcoming, the parent can wait for the next teenage request—the next exchange point. Then the adult might pleasantly reply, "I'm happy to provide what you want, but before that, I need you to do what I've been asking for first."

Saying "No" Is Holding On

Simply put, saying "no" is protecting by objecting. *Holding on* to what one wants or believes, the person states "no" to argue, to protest, to refuse, to reject, to defend, or to block something unwanted from going on.

"No, I disagree!"

"No, that's wrong!"

"No, that's unfair!"

"No, I won't do this!"

"No, I didn't say that!"

"No, stop doing this to me!"

The Necessity of "No"

"No" is a powerful limit-setting word that protects self-interest in relationships. Without the capacity to say no, a young person's well-being can be unguarded. "No" is every person's primary defender, holding on to what matters.

So although "no" may not be popular or easy to say, it is often necessary during the push and shove of adolescence: "I told my boyfriend to stop, he got angry, and now we're not dating anymore!" A no can have social consequences.

It does a teenager no favor to be taught that "no" is the opposite of "nice," to be raised and praised as someone who is always agreeable, never complains, pleases at all costs, goes along to get along, bows to disagreement, and suffers dissatisfaction in silence.

In a world of risks, temptations, and social pressures, parents want to raise a young person sufficiently armed with the power to say no so that safe and healthy self-interest will be protected: "We're glad you stood up against the bullying, even though we're sorry that you had to do it at all."

The Aggravation of "No"

Parents are often less enthusiastic about this negative declaration when it is used with them: "We want our adolescent to be able to say no, just not so often with us!" The adolescent "no" challenges their authority. It opposes what they want.

So, it can be a frustrating adjustment for parents when their mostly compliant (yes-saying) child becomes a more resistant (no-saying) adolescent. Passive resistance, like delay, and active resistance, like argument, can become more frequent: "Her constant disagreement can be exhausting to live with!"

The child grew up in the age of command, believing that parents had the power to force obedience: "My parents are in control." The adolescent, however, has entered the age of consent and now understands that parents can't make or stop them without the young person's cooperation: "To get what they want, my parents need me to go along."

When feeling aggravated by adolescent resistance, parents should remember that the teenager who dares to express no to the family powers that be (parents) is often more practiced with setting limits and saying no to friends: "He's no pushover with us, so we're confident he can stand up to his peers." Saying no can be a stubborn act of holding on to defend well-being.

Also, when feeling frustrated by the adolescent no, it can help to also understand the adolescent's frustration. Pushing for more freedom of operation, the adolescent increasingly encounters the parental no as desired permission or provision is refused: "They never let me do anything!" For an adolescent pushing for more freedom to grow, the limit of a parental no can be hard to take. When an adolescent no is expressed or parental no is challenged, a conversation needs to begin. "No" is often worth talking about.

The Protection of the Parental "No"

Although sometimes angrily accused of being on a power trip by an adolescent whose want has been denied by a parental no, parents often forbid with the young person's welfare in mind. Thus, when giving an important no, parents need to explain their action.

For example, "You are not allowed to drink or otherwise use a drug when you are driving. Here is why. As substance use alters your mood, it affects your mind—your perception, reactivity, and judgment. Driving a car is a very dangerous activity that kills close to 40,000 people a year, so it requires all your sober attention to keep it safe. Any driving you do must be free of alcohol and other drugs."

The Inability to Say "No" to Oneself

"No" can be a statement of determination that can be hard to keep when it means depriving oneself of what one would otherwise like. When *want* overcomes *won't, will* of temptation can rule: "I swore I wouldn't buy anything at the mall, but I let my promise go, so I'll just worry about paying the expense later on." And now credit card debt is impulsively increased by an older adolescent who is still learning hard lessons about managing finances on a limited amount of money.

Even worse, consider the young person who is at the mercy of unhealthy habituation and cravings, unable to say no to powerful urges that entrap her or him in a harmful habituation or dependency: "I know I shouldn't and I swore I wouldn't, but I can't stop myself from doing what feels good, even knowing it is bad for me." Addiction is partly the incapacity to say no to ongoing self-defeating or self-destructive urges. Now therapeutic treatment or assisted abstinence support groups or both may be required to help break compulsion's tenacious hold: "I need help to hold on and say 'no.'"

Divorce: Letting Go While Holding On

A very common family challenge where both letting go and holding on are necessary is *divorce with children*—where the parental challenge is not only to let go of the marriage union but also to hold on to a divided family to which children can still securely belong.

According to the American Psychological Association, about 50 percent of married couples in the United States divorce, with a higher rate of divorce in subsequent marriages. Just as it's hard to marry well with the additional demands and responsibilities of partnership, it's even harder to divorce well when parenthood is involved because now growing child and adolescent lives are affected.

Divorce with children poses a complicated family challenge: how to help them let go the old state of unified family living and how to hold on to continuity of parental care in a divided family life. Consider some basic understandings to accept and parental partnership challenges to be met.

Basic Understandings

Although not as harshly formative as abandonment, abuse, neglect, debilitating illness, or death of a parent, parental divorce is still highly impactful for children and adolescents. One's family before and after divorce is not the same. Adult rejection of the old family unit has taken place, and children and adolescents have a lot of adjustments to make. A core question for children of divorce at any age becomes "What happens to my family now?" Parents need to understand the following:

- Divorce takes children through a painful family change initiated by parents.
- Divorce creates child grief, anger, and anxiety at loss of the unified family.
- Divorce demands adjustment to two-household family living.
- Divorce increases lifestyle differences between parents.
- Divorce means missing one parent when living with the other.
- Divorce shows how loving commitment is not necessarily forever.
- Divorce sets children and adolescents more on their own.
- Divorce can cause closely attached children to cling for more security.
- Divorce can cause detaching adolescents to assert more independence.

In these and other possible ways, it's important for parents to comprehend how their decision to divorce impacts children and adolescents. Sometimes, in determination to move on with their lives, parents can feel frustrated with the child or adolescent whose adjustment and acceptance are taking time to catch up with this painful family change. In general, it's best to be patient and listen to youthful concerns. When parental divorce occurs, children and adolescents more need time; they have some catching up and adjustment to do, with less power to do so than their parents have.

Divorcing Tasks

To let go as partners and live separately, while still holding on together as parents sharing a common concern for their children, is complicated and hard. A functional divorce demands some difficult steps.

Partners must inform children—making sure that children are not blamed for this decision, there is no pressure to take parental sides, and children can ask questions. Unable to do so, unrealistic imaginings can take hold in children's minds.

Partners must separate sharing—who gets what and when, like custody, support, visitation, primary domicile, and educational and health care decision-making. Unable to do so, the relationship can remain opposed and contested.

Partners must emotionally reconcile—coming to terms of emotional acceptance of whatever marital differences grew them apart. Unable to do so, the relationship can remain aggrieved, children torn in between.

Partners must stabilize change—creating two-household living arrangements and a familiar pattern and routines of family living on which children can rely. Unable to do so, life can feel confusing and chaotic.

Partners must recommit as parents—sharing joint concern, cooperation, and communication for the children's welfare. Unable to do so, normal household differences and working together can become divisive.

Divorcing well with children and adolescents, letting go and still holding on, isn't easy. Individual or joint counseling can help the newly unmarried couple meet these objectives.

Divorce with children is not a trivial event. It is emotionally rending and usually takes a year or two for children to adjust to this divisive change. Sometimes there can be lasting effects like distrust in love and reluctance to make commitment. Parents need to be patient while the child or adolescent struggles with the pain of letting go of the unified family unit. Parents must hold on with their unwavering care while everyone grows used to the two-household operation, finally able to grasp this new constellation of family life.

Weaning Adolescents

Just as the young child must be weaned from intimate nursing to feed themselves more independently, so the adolescent must be weaned from dependency on parental support to become a functioning adult. Weaning is like a transfer or handoff, creating willingness to let go of reliance on one's parents to assume more self-sufficiency. Weaning is a basic form of holding on while letting go, hence the title of this book.

Sacrifice is involved on both sides. For the adolescent, greater freedom is burdened by accepting responsibility and enduring resulting hardships. For the parents, the greater loving is to let the loved one go and missing childhood that is dearly remembered.

Specifically, a host of *less/more trade-offs* come into play. For example, the dance of growing separation goes like this:

As we demand less of you, you must demand more of yourself.

As we let go of responsibility, you must assume more.

As we remind you less, you must remember more.

As we contribute less, you must provide more.

As we supervise less, you must manage more.

As we correct less, you must evaluate more.

As we dictate less, you must decide more.

As we fret less, you must worry more.

As we do less, you must do more.

Thus, weaning is how parents and adolescents work themselves out of their traditional relationship—the parent holding on with their love while letting go of governing responsibility so that adolescents can ultimately claim young adult individuality and independence at the end.

Chapter Three

Communicating While Growing Apart

● ● ●

"My parents are harder to talk to now."

Maybe your five-year-old has been at kindergarten while you've been at work. At the end of the day you pick her up and you both enjoy the warmth of a welcome-back hug. Immediately you feel lovingly connected, back in familiar touch, ready to hear what she wants to share. Communication comes easily.

Contrast this reunion with your fifteen-year-old returning from high school after another taxing freshman day, ready for some relief. "How was school?" you ask to show concern. "Okay," she answers, brushing past you to her room, closing the door for time alone, to talk or text with friends. Come adolescence, parental communication with their teenagers often becomes more challenging.

The Change

Why this change? Communication between parent and teenager can increase in complexity as adolescence grows them apart. Increasing separation occurs in their relationship as the young person *differentiates* and *detaches* from childhood and parents in order to express more individuality and assert more independence. As this process unfolds, it's easier now to feel *disconnected* from your teenager who at times becomes more different and distant to get along with than when she or he was still a child.

It's natural to feel they are living worlds apart because increasingly they are. The rapid pace of social, cultural, fashion, and technological change puts even younger parents more out of touch with their emerging adolescent: "The popular music and entertainment are not the same as what we knew and loved!" Generations change. How can each understand what it's like to contend with the demands of their respective ages and stages in life? How can parents understand what a hard day at school is really like? How can the teenager understand what a hard day on the job is really like? Communication matters more than ever because it is the primary means for them to stay connected as healthy separation grows between them.

What follows are some ways to think about communication: what it is, why it is, and how it might helpfully be managed.

Communication Is Sharing Data

Start with a simple definition of communication: sharing personal data of three kinds—about *emotions*, *thoughts*, and *actions*. Even though they've daily lived together in the same family for many years and know each other well on that account, at any moment in time, parent and adolescent are unknowing, in the moment having no sure way to answer three basic questions about each other:

"What are you now *feeling*?"

"What are you now *thinking*?"

"What have you been *doing*?"

Each party has a need for constant data gathering and data sharing so that both parties can be adequately known and stay properly informed. Communication requires talking about oneself and listening to what is being told. Being too inward to speak or too busy to listen can diminish interpersonal knowing.

Unable to obtain answers to these three data questions creates ignorance that can be worrisome. Complains the parent, "Are you upset or in trouble? You don't talk about what's going on!" Not knowing, it's easy to fearfully imagine the worst.

Rather than let ignorance leap to unhappy conclusions, when it comes to communication, it's usually better to check the other person out by requesting more data: "Can you tell me about what's going on? I'm concerned that you may not be okay." *When in doubt, check it out.*

Being unable to convey the three kinds of data and get them heard creates frustration that can cause injury. Complains the teenager, "You don't listen to my feelings, consider my thoughts, or recognize all I do! You don't care to know!" Not being known, it's easy to feel dismissed or discounted.

Rather than let rejection stand and breed resentment at not being heard, when it comes to communication it's usually better to persist for another hearing: "Can I try to tell you again what is really important to me that you know?" *When ignored, keep trying to be heard.*

No matter how close we are to anyone, even with those we know and love the best, in the moment we can remain constant strangers.

For parent and teenager to stay connected through communication, each must do adequate telling and be adequately attentive. Constantly sharing about emotions, thoughts, and actions is required. Routine information-gathering questions are "How are you feeling?" "What's on your mind?" "What's been going on?"

Adequate communication requires cooperation—between a sender of data and a receiver of it. One person sharing a lot but listening little, or one person always listening but seldom sharing, creates inequity in the relationship. At best, each party must be willing and able to do enough of both. "I want to tell about myself and to hear about you."

Sex Differences in Data Sharing

Sometimes, while being accustomed to same-sex friendships growing up, there can be communication differences in data sharing between male and female. Boys can be more used to talking about actions taken with each other and girls more used to talking with each other about shared emotions. In their respective relationships, boy conversation may become more focused on companionship activity, while girl conversation may become more focused on emotional intimacy.

Although this distinction sometimes holds, it can feed the stereotype of the silent man of few words, reluctant to talk about his feelings, and the stereotype of the oversensitive woman, always wanting to discuss her emotions. Confronting disagreement in relationship with each other, such a man may want to immediately talk about what happened and what actions to take, while such a woman may want to immediately focus on the personal impact of what happened and how it felt. Both reactions are worth discussing.

Managing Information Needs

No question: between parent and adolescent, two-way spoken communication counts—regularly exchanging information about feelings, thoughts, and actions to keep each other adequately and accurately informed, sharing and listening to each other's wants and needs, and confronting and resolving normal disagreements.

However, like most truisms, this advice doesn't tell the whole story. It leaves out a lot; conducting spoken communication is more complicated than ongoing sharing of data. There is the matter of managing basic information needs.

Four Information Needs

To appreciate this complexity as it bears on the parent/teenager relationship, consider verbal communication as a mix of meeting *four information needs* that adult and adolescent must continually manage:

- **The need to know**—for curiosity: "I want to find out about this."
- **The need not to know**—for ignorance: "I don't want to hear about that."
- **The need to be known**—for intimacy: "I want to be truly understood."
- **The need not to be known**—for privacy: "I don't want to reveal everything."

Consider these four information needs one at a time.

The Need to Know—"I Want to Find Out About This."

Verbal communication is primarily concerned with exchanging data about feelings, thoughts, and behaviors. Parental curiosity about their teenager is constantly interested in all three kinds of information.

"If I know your emotions, then I can give sensitive support."

"If I know your thoughts, then I can understand your reasoning."

"If I know about your actions, then I can keep up with what you're doing."

This expression of interest is not just the parents' way; the teenager also needs to be kept up to date on them. Sometimes parents are so caught up in their child's life that they inadequately disclose about themselves: "I want to know about your day, but I don't want to talk about mine." Years ago, when I asked an eighteen-year-old to tell me about his parents, the young man replied, "I can't tell you that much." "Why is that?" I asked. "You've lived with them all your life." His answer: "Because most of what we ever talked about was me." What a waste! Most of what parents give their child is who and how they are, and the young person learns a lot from hearing about the adults' experience. In their preoccupation to satisfy the need to know about their teenager, adults can neglect the teenager's need to know about them.

Parents often want assurance that teenagers will tell important kinds of information about themselves. Parents might state the following: "Whenever you're stuck, confused, overwhelmed, in doubt, in pain, in trouble, in danger, scared, feel unwell, or are seriously unhappy, please let us know so we can be there for you." Of course, if parents want to know, they must be safe to tell. Criticism, blame, upset, or overreactions can reduce the likelihood of being told.

The Need Not to Know—"I Don't Want to Hear About That."

No parent wants a daily transcript of all that's going on in the adolescent's inner and outer worlds: "You don't have to tell us everything, just the important things." The more they're told, the more parents have to think and maybe worry about. Or consider the teenager who is continually offered chapter and verse of the parent's unhappy job experience: "I don't want to hear how bad your day at work was every day!"

Then there are parental warnings about adolescent risk-taking that the teenager may not want to hear. "Stop telling me! If I considered everything that could go wrong I'd never try anything!" Denial of danger sometimes enables acts of everyday risking and daring. Denial presents young people with the freedom to proceed unmindfully: "It's not a problem." "It's not that dangerous." "I know enough to stay okay." "If I'm careful, I won't get hurt." "It won't happen to me!"

There's no point in arguing with a teenager's need not to know, as denial won't let in any cautionary data. "I won't listen to what you're saying!" "You don't know what you're talking about!" But denial doesn't make threats go away; it can amplify danger by encouraging ignorance.

So, if parents are concerned with some harmful possibility in their teenager's life, instead of trying to scare the young person away from danger with alarm, expressing concern for the adolescent's well-being and explaining why can be a better approach. "To reduce the possibility of car accidents and harm when driving, don't text when you drive and always buckle up."

The Need to Be Known—"I Want to Be Truly Understood."

Individual change can be estranging in a relationship when one party doesn't grasp the transformation the other is growing through. At such times the changing person can feel disconnected, lonely, and misunderstood.

You can see this when a child enters adolescence and the parents, who used to be so knowing of the little girl or boy, seem now not to comprehend what is happening. In ignorance, parents wonder, or even ask, "What's wrong with you? You're so disorganized and distracted now. You live in a mess and can't remember anything!" For the young teenager, overwhelmed by physical and social changes, one compelling gift of adolescent peers is how they can relate to what it's like to be that age right now. "My friends understand me when my parents don't!" As for parents, struggling to adjust, they often experience more impatience, uncertainty, and anxiety.

With the onset of adolescence, both parent and teenager can feel more estranged as the coming-of-age passage changes the child—and the parent in response—and alters the old relationship between them. To keep up with these changes, each is now more in need of more understanding. Thus, adequately sharing and truly listening to each other is what both need to do. In addition, when conversation feels awkward or uncomfortable, when words are hard to find, sometimes creating companionship around a common need or enjoyment can suffice to maintain closeness. "Let's just grab something to eat and take in a movie." Doing things together even without much talking is still a good way of being together.

The Need Not to Be Known—"I Don't Want to Reveal Everything."

The older the adolescent, the more private her or his more independent world becomes. Privacy protects freedom from being fully known. "What I choose to tell is up to me." Thus, while the child may welcome parental questions as expressions of older interest, the adolescent may see them in less favorable terms—as invasive of privacy and emblematic of adult authority. "Stop asking me about so much!"

But if parents have a powerful need to know, what else can they do?

They can explain their need to know. Short of making a request, but better than abrupt questions, parents can explain their interest: "The reason I'm asking is not to pry but from concern for your safety. If we know where you are, and you know we know where you are, then we can be there for you should a need for help arise."

Information Needs Conflict

The four information needs that communication satisfies for parent and adolescent can be summarized as follows:

- For *curiosity* and *the need to know*: the desire to stay adequately informed and up to date in a constantly changing world.
- For *denial* and *the need not to know*: the desire to limit possible knowledge in a world of infinitely disturbing or distracting news.
- For *intimacy* and *the need to be known*: to be closely understood in a world where casual and superficial relationships are more the rule.
- For *privacy* and *the need not to be known*: to have some concealment in a personal world where others cannot intrude.

Then there are common communication conflicts between information needs, such as the need to know against the need not to be known. Parent: "Tell us everything!" Teenager: "I'll tell you some, but not all." And there is the need to be known against the need not to know. Parents: "We want to tell you why we are divorcing!" Teenager: "I don't want to know who did what to whom!" Managing information needs can be tricky.

Predictable emotional discomfort can sometimes signify when an information need is being frustrated. In this regard, feelings can be good informants.

- Frustrate your need to know, and you can feel anxious and worried.
- Frustrate your need not to know, and you can feel overloaded and stressed.
- Frustrate your need to be known, and you can feel ignored and estranged.
- Frustrate your need not to be known, and you can feel exposed and threatened.

Spoken communication is often clumsy, but it remains the best tool for maintaining a parent/teenager relationship. The adequate exchange of information matters, so how to manage this mix of knowing and not knowing, of being known and not being known, is well worth talking about with your adolescent, not just for your caring relationship, but for other caring relationships to come.

Clarifying Meaning

At a workshop many years ago, psychologist Dr. John Narciso (his 1975 book is *Declare Yourself*) introduced me to the idea of *operational communication—talking not in generalities but in terms of specific behaviors, actions, happenings, and events.* What follows is my take on this concept when working with the parent/teenager relationship.

Categorical communication—statements of a general nature meant to communicate a lot but that actually communicate very little—has pitfalls. For example, I could ask a group of parents at a workshop what major ways they would like their adolescent to act with them at home. Among the common categorical answers that everyone might agree upon are "responsible," "respectful," and "reliable."

Then I would ask the operational question: "Could one of you join me up front and *do* responsible, and *do* respectful, and *do* reliable with me?" No takers. Why not? The problem is that categories lack specific meaning. Too vague, they often have little applied use. When parents are in a hurry, for example, they often use the shorthand of categorical communication in the often-mistaken belief that the teenager will know exactly what they mean, when the young person often does not. "Just be careful. That's all I'm asking." The parent is expressing concern but not offering any specificity.

To be better understood, parents need to *operationalize* their choice of language by talking in terms of actions, behaviors, happenings, and events; for example:

"By *responsible* I mean that you will tell me the truth."

"By *respectful* I mean listening and not interrupting when I'm talking."

"By *reliable* I mean you will keep your promises and agreements with me."

This is why parents need *not* to tell their nine-year-old early adolescent to "clean up" her or his room. Agreeably, the young person may comply with the parental request and then after ten minutes declare, "Job done!" However, on inspection the parent finds all manner of belongings snuck beneath bedcovers, shoved under the bed, piled in the corners, and thrown into the closet. "This isn't cleaned up!" the parents object. "You've just hidden the mess!" But to the young person's eye, "It looks clean to me!"

So now, after the fact, the parent has to translate the categorical instruction. They do so by using operational language to specify what they meant. "By 'clean up' we mean the stuff to be thrown away goes in the wastebasket, play objects are put back on shelves, dirty clothes go in the hamper, clean clothes are in drawers or in bins or hung up, and no hiding disorder where it can't be seen."

Of course, the young adolescent can be confusingly categorical too, like when complaining to parents, "You're not being *fair*, *friendly*, or *fun* to live with anymore!" Now the parent needs some operationalizing of terms to understand exactly what's on the young person's mind, what she or he is specifically meaning.

In sum, when communicating with your adolescent, try being operational and not categorical. Clarify your communication this way, and you'll encourage your teenager to do the same with you. In general, the more emotionally aroused the communicators become, the more reliance on categorical language often occurs as generalities and labeling become tempting to use.

It can take discipline in heated conversations to stick to operational specifics, but it definitely helps. "Instead of complaining how we don't really care, tell us specifically what you would like us to do and not do that would cause you to believe our caring was there."

Communication and Emotional Intensity

Compared with childhood closeness, growing changes can now stress the parent/daughter or parent/son relationship as more distance and differences gradually expand between them.

In consequence, parent and teenager can find each other more emotionally intense with each other, particularly during normal disagreements that increasingly occur. For example, the adolescent can become more frustrated and angry when not getting the desired freedom, while the parents can become more offended and worried over the growing changes, not liking or understanding what is going on.

Appreciating Emotion

Start by recognizing the importance of emotion in human functioning. From my perspective, emotions are part of everyone's *affective awareness system* that helps them *feel* when something significant is happening in their internal or external world of experience that deserves attention.

Each kind of emotional awareness focuses on a different aspect of life experience. For example, on the hard side, *fear* warns of danger, *anger* responds to violation, *frustration* identifies blockage, and *grief* testifies to loss. On the happier side, *love* affirms devotion, *joy* celebrates fulfillment, *pride* enjoys accomplishment, and *curiosity* expresses interest.

Without access to their emotion, people lack important self-awareness: "I don't know how I feel. I don't know what's going on with me." Our emotions help keep us in touch with our well-being.

However, *while emotions can be very good informants, they can be very bad advisers.* Thinking with one's feelings can get people into all kinds of difficulty. For example, *yielding to infatuation* can lead a young person into accepting dangerous attention; *retaliating in anger* can make a hostile situation hurtful; *avoiding a scary challenge* can limit opportunity for growth or empower a bully.

Between parent and adolescent, it's important to honor the message emotion brings when, for example, feeling *disappointed* by the other person's reaction. In this case, rather than impulsively following emotion's unhappy advice and charge, "You're never there for me!" the relationship is better served by taking a deep breath and relying on judgment to respond, "I'd like to talk about how I was hoping you would respond." *The safe management of strong emotions requires the discipline of self-restraint so the concerns can be rationally discussed.*

Emotional Extortion

While feelings express emotional states, they can be used as powerful persuaders, as the little child learns when dealing with the giant caretakers who rule her or his world. Think of the persuasive, expressive tactics the preverbal child learns to use to get attention and their way with parents. The hug, the smile, the laugh, the frown, the cry, the hit, the tantrum, and the scream all emotionally communicate what is or is not wanted. "He lets us know when he's unhappy by acting loud or sad." "She knows how to charm her way with us with her smile."

Come the child's early acquisition of spoken language, parents encourage the transition from acting out to talking to express what is wanted or not wanted. "Instead of hitting to show what you dislike, use your feeling words to say what you want so I can understand."

Sometimes, however, older children, adolescents, and adults can be tempted, particularly in disagreement, to use the expression of strong emotion to gain influence. They can offer the continuation of good feelings or cessation of hard feelings for some concession from the other person to get what they want.

A few common methods of emotional extortion are as follows.

Sulking: "To restore my spirits, give me my way."

Suffering: "To heal my pain, give me my way."

Anger: "To stop my being mad, give me my way."

Rejection: "To have my company, give me my way."

Blame: "To be forgiven, give me my way."

Apathy: "To have me care, give me my way."

Pity: "To ease my plight, give me my way."

Love: "To regain my affection, give me my way."

Any use of emotional extortion is a bad bargain because it corrupts the honest expression of intense feelings and lowers trust by using them for manipulative gain. "You're just acting hurt to get what you want." "You're just acting loving to win me over." "You're just joking to avoid serious discussion." Parents need to avoid such behavior, and should not give in if an adolescent employs it with them.

On these occasions, simply declare to your teenager, "Instead of using your feelings to get your way, please specifically state what it is you want or do not want to have happen and we can talk about that."

Staying Calm

One important challenge of parenting an adolescent is honoring hard or hot feelings with acceptance without indulging them with action. When stressed, surprised, or upset, exercise the adult maturity of self-restraint.

When in disagreement, when criticized, when faced with the unexpected from the teenager, it can take effort not to lose one's cool or temper, not to end up pouring on the emotional fire with inflammatory language like criticism, blame, threat, or name-calling. Acting upset with your upset teenager only results in more upset. Yelling at her to stop yelling only encourages yelling by adult example. Because conflict encourages similarity this way, model behavior that you want the young person to imitate. Don't let the teenager's urgency trap you in a *tyranny of now*: "I need to know right this minute!" No. If you feel emotionally pressured, take a break and explain to your impatient teenager that you need some time for thought before deciding. Then reflect and ask yourself, "What do I feel like saying and doing?" and "What do I think is wise to say and do?"

Then choose the second over the first.

Communication Is Speaking Up

Sometimes parents miss the more willing compliance of childhood and weary of the increased resistance that can come with adolescence: "Stop arguing!" "Don't talk back!" "Just do what you're told!"
"I don't want to hear another word!" "'Now' doesn't mean later!" In
this way communication as "speaking up" can be given a bad name.
Such parents may prefer a young person who shuts up and simply
complies without raising a question or making an objection.

However, disagreement and argument are functional. They are
informing and engaging. They encourage discussion. Silence communicates nothing specific and can be interpreted in many ways. It
fosters ignorance and can be estranging. In the family, where formative patterns of communication are learned, *it's in the young person's
long-term interests to be encouraged to practice the skills of speaking
up.* What results can speaking up have for adolescents?

- **Speaking up can disclose state of mind and feeling.** Do parents want to raise a silent or verbally expressive child?

- **Speaking up can explain perception.** Do parents want to raise
  a child who defers to others or who declares a personal point
  of view?

- **Speaking up can encourage questioning to understand.** Do
  parents want to raise a child who waits to be told or one who
  asks to find out?

- **Speaking up can take a stand.** Parents can ask themselves: do
  they want to raise a child who silently accepts what feels wrong
  or one who objects to unfairness?

- **Speaking up can resolve differences.** Do parents: want to raise a child who avoids disagreement or one who engages to talk it out?

At issue in family communication is how socially outspoken or socially silent a young person is encouraged to be. In my opinion, *to graduate a shutting-up teenager from parental care does not serve a young person well.* To make one's way in the world, speaking up is an essential life skill, as is knowing how to do so in a respectful way.

Keeping a Healthy Perspective

I've been asked, "If you had one piece of advice to give parents with teenagers, what would it be?" My answer: "Keep a healthy perspective."

By "perspective" I mean the mental set that parents maintain to decide what matters most and what matters least, what is major and what is minor, what to confront and what to ignore in their teenager's life. Perspective shapes the vision they have, which affects the actions they take.

It can get complicated: "Right now doing her exercises to rehab the injury is more important than keeping her room regularly picked up." Perspective can shift priorities as circumstances change.

Then parents can disagree: "It's no big deal!" or "It could be very serious!" And now they discuss downplaying or enlarging what happened with their teenager to reach a compromise perspective both can support.

While a child certainly gives parents much to keep track of, an adolescent gives them even more. Growing up complicates the young person's life as she or he pushes for more room to grow—for freedom of action to develop independence and for freedom of definition to express individuality.

To maintain a healthy parental perspective during their child's coming-of-age transformation of girl into young woman or boy into young man, parents have to focus on the big things, not make big things out of small things, and give small things the attention they deserve.

Big and Small Things

While parents differ on what constitute big parts of their teenager's life, consider nine dimensions of growth a parent might want to monitor: emotional well-being, self-acceptance, physical health, personal safety, academic effort, peer companionship, family membership, individual responsibility, and social compliance.

Big problems that go unattended often get worse. So, when any of these dimensions of young life become troubled, that's a big thing to attract parents' attention.

Because adolescence can be more challenging than childhood for a girl or boy, it can be a more challenging passage for parents as well. By comparison, the younger child felt simpler and easier for them to live with.

For example, now they may have to contend with a young person who is more frequently argumentative—or forgetful, distracted, disorganized, restless, discontent, messy, self-preoccupied, secretive, uncommunicative, resistant, impulsive, irritable, critical, unappreciative, or some combination of these normal changes.

In response, it can be harder for parents to remain calm, cool, and collected with their teenager. However, when they lose their patience or temper, parents can lose perspective and overreact, in the process making a large issue over a small matter: "That's it! I've had it! Coming home to your dirty dishes in the kitchen after a long day at work is not okay! It just shows how irresponsible you are!" Now a messy sink is treated like a serious character flaw.

As mentioned, although very good informants about significant goings-on in their inner and outer worlds of experience, emotions can be very bad advisers when parents start thinking with their feelings. They are better served using their judgment to cope. Adult maturity and self-discipline need to come into play to keep normal adolescent changes from inflaming parental perspective and turning minor irritations into major offenses.

Respecting Small Things

Then there is the need for sensitivity. Parents can do certain little things to make a big positive difference in the relationship with their teenager because those little things can represent so much when regularly given and make a big negative difference when they're not. *Small events can have symbolic power.* For example,

- **Smiling** expresses warmth. Not given: "You never look happy to see me!"
- **Listening** gives worth to what is said. Not given: "You never hear me out!"
- **Appreciating** honors efforts made. Not given: "You never even thank me!"
- **Courtesy** shows consideration. Not given: "You never just ask me first!"
- **Memory** keeps in mind. Not given: "You never remember promises!"
- **Apologizing** truly regrets. Not given: "You never say you're sorry!"

- **Noticing** pays attention. Not given: "You never see when I do well!"
- **Assisting** offers help. Not given: "You never lend me a hand!"
- **Compliments** value. Not given: "You never praise me!"
- **Empathy** supports. Not given: "You never care!"
- **Hugs** affirm. Not given: "You never like me!"

To maintain parental perspective, don't shy away from dealing with the big things. Don't emotionally make small things larger than they are. And don't forget how little acts can matter. Because they can signify so much, small things are often big things in disguise. Thus, forgetting or reneging on a simple promise can result in a loss of trust and create instability.

The Power of Promises

Promises are communications that matter a lot. There are two overlapping promises that parents need to typically increase when their child enters adolescence. One need is for the young person to tell them the truth. The other need is for the young person to keep commitments to them.

A promise is verbal assurance that a commitment has been made and will be kept. In this sense, all promises incur obligation. They are contractual in this way.

A promise can be a powerful commitment . It can verbally *verify* the occurrence of something past or present—what actually happened. And it can *vow* to desist from hereon or to deliver at some specified future time—what won't be repeated or what will occur. At a period of more development, change, and uncertainty, adolescent promises kept to parents can count for a lot: "I appreciate how you keep your word. Now I have one less thing to worry about."

So, after a troubling incident, parents may want both kinds of promises from their wayward teenager. Verification: "Do you promise that this is how it really was?" Vow: "Do you promise not to do this again?"

Broken promises can prove costly. At worst, they can betray a relationship: "You swore you'd never do that and you did!"

Promises as Commitments

Promises are powerful. Keeping your promise shows that you have acted as you said you would, that you have kept your pledge, and that your word is good. The power of a promise kept is that it creates reliability, predictability, and security to be counted on, thus engendering trust in the relationship. An adult example would be a couple exchanging marriage vows that they commit to keep. Both parties make promises on which the other can depend. Promise-keeping between parent and child and parent and adolescent is just as important.

Breaking a promise indicates unreliability, unpredictability, and untrustworthiness. Other people can feel surprised, disappointed, and betrayed: "I thought I could count on you!" "You let me down!" "You misled me!" If parents want to *encourage* promise-keeping in their teenager, they have to *model* promise-keeping—which consistent parents tend to do, but which inconsistent parents often do not.

"Sometimes my parents promise something bad will happen if I don't do what they want. Then they forget, get tired, or become busy, and just let it go." In this case, a teenager may bet that parents don't really think the promised rules and regulations they make are important, they're testing to see if some warning or requirement is real. Parental rules and regulations only have power to the degree they are commitments kept.

One ongoing parenting commitment that matters is to hold the adolescent accountable for consequences of choices made.

Claiming Consequences

During adolescence, the teenager gathers increased freedom of experience, becomes less dependent on parents, and learns to function more on her or his own terms. But what is the core experience that parents are working with here?

I believe it is the *choice/consequence connection*. What parents must help the self-determined adolescent keep in mind is that every "free" choice she or he makes comes with baggage in the form of consequences and thus is never entirely "free" at all. This choice/consequence connection has two empowering values: for *responsibility* and for *instruction*.

- When a young person owns their share in the outcome of a personal choice, they accept some *responsibility*: "If I had chosen differently, none of this would have happened." "To get what I wanted, I had to work very hard."

- When a young person's choice is informed by the consequence that follows, then that outcome can have *instructional value*: "At least I know more now than I did before." "Going through all that taught me a lot."

Sometimes the young person may not feel inclined or able to link choice to consequence.

- The adolescent may *not see* the connection. *Ignorance*: "I didn't know I shouldn't until I got suspended." Parent: "Better to check out the rules than to learn the hard way."

- The adolescent may *not admit* the connection. *Denial:* "I didn't want to think this could happen if I wasn't careful!" Parent: "Lots of things are riskier than we'd like them to be."
- The adolescent may *not care* about the connection. *Apathy:* "So what if not studying lowers my grades?" Parent: "What feels like it doesn't matter now can matter a lot to you later on."
- The adolescent may *not feel able to stop* the connection. *Habit:* "I can't keep from doing this to myself!" Parent: "If you can't quit on your own, maybe help is needed."

Teenage statements that disown or discount the choice/consequence connection can be frustrating, even alarming for parents: "What is it going to take for you to learn from your mistakes and not keep repeating them?" "How can you not see what you are doing to yourself?"

Sometimes, only repeat encounters with unhappy consequences finally convince a young person to acknowledge the linkage and consider making different choices with better outcomes. Consider this summer job education: "Lateness to work got me fired again. If I want to keep a job, I'll have to get up and show up on time."

Unwanted consequences of unwise choices can be positively persuasive when what they communicate has lasting instructional value: "Experience is the toughest teacher I've ever had!"

However, for acquiring the basics of communication, parents remain the primary instructors.

Parents Teach Communication

The fundamental human relations skill is managing communication. By example, interaction, and instruction, communication is what parents powerfully teach: the daily use of the spoken word. This expression enables so many parts of life. Communication is how you

- Convey meaning.
- Gather information.
- Know from listening.
- Are known from telling.
- Cooperate with others.
- Influence outcomes.
- Keep relationships connected.
- Make your way in the world.
- Create commonalities.
- Resolve differences.
- Sustain intimacy.
- Express caring.

When it comes to learning and practicing so many functions of communication, at home, in the family, with parents is where this invaluable part of the adolescent's education begins. ●

Chapter Four

The Importance of Heeding Freedom's Call

● ● ●

"Freedom's just another name for doing what I want."

At times, there's something almost patriotic about adolescence, about the young person bravely pushing for more liberation with resolve and resistance and sometimes risking disapproval from parents, the ruling authorities for setting family terms. This push for growing freedom can give the teenager a more rebellious reputation than the child had.

Freedom denied can be frustrating for both parties when neither can get their way. For the parent, timely compliance can feel harder to get, while for the teenager, desired permission can feel harder to gain. It's easier for both to become frustrated in the relationship. For the teenager, freedom from parental regulation and freedom for self-direction are compelling. For the parents, freedom to set terms for safe and responsible conduct is part of their job. So from time to time there can be more conflict between the adolescent need for freedom and the parental need to determine what's allowed. "I want to try this!" can conflict with "You're not ready yet!"

Best to accept this tension as meant to be.

Two Freedom Goals

I believe adolescent growth is developmentally driven by two *freedom goals*—for *detachment to gain more independence* and *differentiation to claim more individuality.*

To detach from childhood and parents, some common markers occur.

- The company of peers competes with spending time with family: "I want my social life with friends."
- Privacy from parents is increasingly protected: "I want my parents to leave me more alone."
- Life outside of home in the larger world becomes more compelling: "I want to spend more time apart from family."
- Asserting more personal direction feels empowering: "I want what I do left up to me."

By the end of adolescence, a *functional independence* is claimed: "I can lead my life and take care of myself."

To *differentiate* from childhood and family, common markers occur.

- There is more trying out ways of believing and behaving: "I want to become different than I used to be."
- It feels like there is less similarity and more contrast with parents: "We're becoming less alike than we used to be."

- Personal expression is more influenced by peers: "I want to keep up with what matters to friends."
- Personal interests are pursued intensively: "I want to spend more time doing what's important to me."

By the end of adolescence, a *fitting definition* is claimed: "I understand and am truly my own person now."

Achieving both goals, the young person can claim both agency and identity. "What I do and who I am are up to me!"

This development is not an overnight transformation. It takes many trial-and-error choices over time, from mastery learning (how to do) and mistake-based education (how not to do). This transformation unfolds over ten to twelve years, usually coming to completion a little after the college-age period is over.

Adolescence Feels Freer Than Childhood

Come adolescence, the young person feels increased power of choice in two important ways.

First, the child lived in the *age of command*, believing parental authority required strict obedience: "I must do as I'm told." The adolescent, however, has entered the *age of consent*, now knowing that parents can't make or stop the young person without her or his cooperation: "What I choose to do or not do for you is basically up to me."

And second, where the child lived in the *age of confiding*, believing that parents should strictly be told the truth, the adolescent enters an *age of concealment*, as privacy from parents becomes powerful: "My parents must depend on what I say to know what's really going on." And now there is more strategic reporting, more selective disclosure, and sometimes more lying.

Why Surrender Freedom to Parents?

The adolescent feels empowered by freedom in ways the child did not. And yet, despite this growing awareness of personal freedom from consent and concealment, why do most adolescents choose to give parents as much cooperative compliance and forthright communication as they do?

In the case of consent, the young person continues to want the protection of family structure and parental oversight: "I still want to follow their lead." And in the case of confiding, the young person still wants to feel closely connected to and truthfully known by parents. Love for and trust from parents is persuasive: "I still want their knowing and care."

Also, dependence on parents' supervision can feel supportive. An early-adolescent example would be the truly distracted sixth-grader who declares, "I'd never get my homework done if my parents didn't keep after me, even though I don't like it when they do." So parents provide some of the nightly motivation that the young person at the moment lacks: "His homework is our homework until he can get it done without us."

Or denial of parents' permission can sometimes feel protective. A later example would be the teenager still wanting parents to make choices for her, while resenting them for so doing. Consider the case of the high school junior who has been asked by an older guy to her first college party. While she is flattered to receive this more grown-up invitation, she feels emotionally and socially unready to go. However, she is also reluctant to refuse on her own behalf. So when her parents say, "No," she jumps all over them, "You never let me do anything!" Blaming them to excuse her refusal, she saves face, but is grateful they made a choice she felt unable to freely make for herself: "Thank goodness they wouldn't let me go!" She gives consent to their control because it helps keep her life within safe and tolerable bounds. There are helpful times when parents can decide about the hard choices the adolescent lacks the willpower to make.

Sometimes privacy can feel painfully isolating. An example of the teenager still giving up precious privacy to be known by parents might be the sad student who has just been jilted by his first crush in middle school. Unwilling to show how hurt he feels, he acts unfazed, and his parents believe his lie. As far as they know he is just suffering from a passing case of lost "puppy love." Then late one evening, he confides to them what is really happening emotionally. He is unhappy enough to have thoughts about hurting himself. He is worried about what he might do. While a private part of him doesn't want to be known, a lonely part of him wants an empathetic connection to them, which, once informed, they immediately provide. Intimacy with parents can secure their emotional support. At a painful time, he wants to be truly known.

Discussing Freedom

Parents may generally want to encourage some adolescent freedoms, like taking responsibility, speaking up, and asserting self-discipline, for example. They may want to discourage others, like entertainment escape at the expense of task engagement, procrastinating and being too late, and rule breaking for illicit freedom, for example.

An ongoing part of the parental job is monitoring teenage choice-making, measuring out more freedom as they think wise, appreciating decisions that work well, and addressing decisions that do not. All the while, parents must understand that everyone, including themselves, has a mixed record of wise and unwise decision-making: "We make our mistakes too."

Since freedom is opportunity for choice-making, what might parents explain about this challenging experience? Consider a few things they might say, all tending to the same conclusion: *how freedom often isn't free.*

- **Choices can be shortsighted.** "You thought about the fun but not the danger."
- **Choices can take effort.** "It can be really hard to make up your mind."
- **Choices can be a gamble.** "Maybe you'll get some of what you want, but maybe you won't."
- **Choices can build habits.** "When you decided to do this, you increased the likelihood of doing so again."
- **Choices can create responsibility.** "Now you must deal with the result of your decision."
- **Choices can educate.** "Because of the outcome, you know what to do and not to do again."
- **Choices can be revealing.** "How you decided expressed a lot about who you are."
- **Choices can matter.** "What you decide in the present can influence future possibilities."
- **Choices can be thoughtless.** "Thinking with your feelings can overrule better judgment."
- **Choosing can reduce other choices.** "When you decide on this, you can no longer do that."
- **Choices can create surprises.** "No matter what you planned, you can still get the unexpected."

When the teenager starts wanting more freedom, then it's worthwhile to talk about what the young person is really asking for. This is not a theoretical discussion to have; it is a practical one because the young person's growing life is at stake. Parents can explain, "Freedom is complicated because making choices is complicated, so take the time to think about what you want, choose as wisely as you can, and learn from in-life education, from what worked well, and from what you may not want to do again."

For the older adolescent, this mature understanding of freedom of personal choice is sobering. Thus you can appreciate this sense of disenchantment a young person often experiences when she or he physically moves out of the family home and functional independence finally begins. *What a bummer! Freedom's not as great as I thought it would be. Now there's more I have to do and less being done for me. In a lot of ways, I was freer living at home!*

Readiness for Freedom

Adolescence is a gathering of personal power, and "freedom" is that power's name.

When it comes to granting requests for adolescent freedom, parents have to judge whether their teenager is ready to manage this increased latitude of choice. For example, their middle school student wants permission to roam the city with friends on weekends, or their high school junior wants permission to have an after-school job, fifteen hours a week.

Now they want time to think in terms of current performance: "This is what we need from you before we will consider more freedom that you need from us." Parents can treat the granting of more freedom as *contractual*. What self-management behaviors is the teenager bringing to the table that parents might find persuasive?

Some desirable behaviors to include in this contract might be as follows:

Forethought. "You take the time to think ahead before you go ahead. You don't simply act impulsively."

Honesty. "You give us adequate and accurate information. You don't withhold or distort the truth."

Commitment. "You keep your promises and agreements with us. You don't break your word."

Responsibility. "You take care of business at home, at school, and elsewhere. You don't neglect the basics."

Exchange. "You live on two-way terms, doing for us like we do for you. You don't only consider yourself."

Communication. "You are willing to discuss our concerns when they arise. You don't refuse to listen or to talk."

Courtesy. "You treat us with caring and respect. You don't act in insulting or unfriendly ways."

"Live up to these terms, and we are more likely to consider new freedoms you want. However, if you act thoughtlessly, if you lie, if you break promises, if you neglect obligations, if you act like only your needs matter, if you are not available to talk, if you act disrespectfully or hurtfully when you do, then we will be less likely to allow freedoms that you want."

To some degree, when it comes to allowing more personal freedom, the adolescent has to make her or his case. One dad described this as *evidence-based parenting*, "When you want some new freedom, convince us by showing how well you're handling your life right now."

Preparing for Independence

Since an adolescent is partly an adult-in-training, the primary trainers are parents, who are always in the business of anticipating more freedom of independence to come. Their challenge is to help in this preparation.

For example, consider the parents' *readiness curriculum* for their teenager who has just entered high school. Now parents have just *forty-eight short months* to prepare their teenager with enough self-management capacity to support more functional independence that increases after graduation day. Preparation requires thinking ahead and is a parental responsibility.

So, with their entering high school freshman, parents might think ahead about empowering their teenager with necessary *exit skills* to support their independence. Parents can ask themselves, *Over the next four years, what grown-up competencies do we rely on that we can teach our teenager? What can she or he can practice now so that they have the smallest next step to independent functioning after graduating from our daily care?*

For example, parents can decide when during the high school years they are going to start teaching money management skills like earning, saving, credit usage, buying, budgeting, banking, and bill paying. Although some parents may feel uncomfortable letting the teenager understand the specifics of their finances—what is earned, saved, charged, owed, paid, and spent—opening the household books so the young person can understand monthly money management decisions required to support a family can be powerfully instructive: "Because we have a limited income, deciding what *not* to buy is an important part of managing our money."

Or with their fifth-grader they train the child to use a calendar to get in the habit of tracking homework assignments and tests in preparation for middle school: "Next year at school will become more complicated. You will have to juggle instructional tasks and longer assignments from multiple teachers. So we want you to practice now for later. Learning to keep a calendar will help you stay organized for when there will be much more demand to keep track of."

Freedom to Fail

Sometimes an adolescent fears venturing into a new area of freedom because the parental response to any mistake or misdeed is a severely disapproving one: "What's the matter with you anyway? At your age you should know better by now!" Intolerant of errors, the parent can resort to criticism to discourage repetition. In doing so, however, their disapproval can make freedom and accepting responsibility riskier for the teenager to take: "I'd rather not try than get put down when I mess up."

In general, when teenage errors occur, it works best when parents honor *mistake-based education*. They might explain something like this:

"Everybody makes mistakes. A mistake is a choice people would make differently if they could do it over again. People don't make mistakes because they want to; they make mistakes because they didn't know any better or didn't think more clearly at the time. All mistakes are costly, but they can be worth the expense if they are used to inform and instruct. A bad mistake can teach a good lesson. Making a mistake is not a failing; not learning from a mistake is a failing. It is ignorant to make a mistake, but it is stupid to repeat a mistake. Sometimes people have to repeat the same mistake a number of times when there is something hard they don't want to learn before they finally stop acting senseless and wise up. The smartest people are not those who never make mistakes but those who use mistakes to make better choices the next time around. The stupidest people are those who are unable or unwilling to admit mistakes out of the wrong belief that no one should ever make a mistake."

For example, consider the seventeen-year-old, head hung low, slumped over, in counseling with his father, sad about having screwed up again. He was feeling like a failure in the man's eyes. Then his dad said an uplifting thing,

"Son, as far as I'm concerned, if you're not making some mistakes, that just means you're not trying hard enough. As an adult who continues to fumble his way through life, I believe the main thing is to take your lumps when you slip up. Don't beat yourself up. Just learn the hard way and then carry on knowing more than you did before." And then his son straightened up and sadly smiled, "Thanks, Dad. I needed to hear that!"

Freedom to Learn

If parents want their adolescent to feel free to learn from education and life experience in order to grow, then like the father quoted above, they need to respect the *risks of learning*, of which the adolescent is often painfully aware. For example, consider this common difference.

After instructing a lesson, the teacher asks a question: "Who knows the answer? Raise your hand, and I will call on one of you." In the first-grade classroom many arms frantically wave to get chosen: "Me! Me! Me!" However, in the seventh-grade classroom, hands are more reluctantly raised and more silence rules. Why the contrast? I believe that, beginning at ages nine to thirteen, the self-consciousness that accompanies early adolescence is often the answer. Now a young person, feeling beset by puberty and easily embarrassed, can feel more at risk of learning than did the confident, sheltered child. What risks? Think of them this way.

While learning builds self-esteem, it also takes self-esteem to learn, particularly in the form of confidence. Therefore, parents as the primary teachers of their less self-assured adolescent need to free up learning by doing what they can to make common risks of learning safe, or else it can feel safer not to try.

Consider five common adolescent risks of learning and parental responses that can work badly or well.

- **An adolescent may declare ignorance:** *"I don't know."* In response, an intolerant, unsafe parent might say, "Are you stupid?" A safe parent would say, "All learning starts by admitting what we don't understand."
- **An adolescent may make mistakes:** *"I messed up."* In response, an impatient, unsafe parent might say, "You got it wrong again!" A safe, accepting parent would say, "Getting it wrong is how you learn to get right."
- **An adolescent may feel dumb:** *"I'm not getting it!"* In response, a frustrated, unsafe parent might say, "What's the matter with you?" A safe, empathetic parent would say, "You're not being slow. You're learning at your own rate."
- **An adolescent may look foolish:** *"Others will think less of me!"* In response, an unsafe, critical parent might say, "This just shows how slow you are!" A safe parent would say, "Letting others see you struggle is a brave thing to do!"
- **An adolescent may get a bad evaluation:** *"I'm going to fail!"* In response, an unsafe, dismissive parent might say, "You'll never learn!" A safe parent would say, "Even getting it wrong, you'll know more than you did before."

The capacity to grow partly depends on the adolescent's felt freedom to learn, so parents need to do their part in making normal risks of learning safe. Thus, in addition to monitoring their own behavior, they keep their home a tease-free zone. From parents and among siblings, no sarcasm or put-downs are allowed. Those who know are not allowed to criticize the ignorant, make fun of the younger, or ridicule the attempts of the insecure.

Ambivalence About Freedom

While freedom is prized in adolescent life, I believe the picture of a purely freedom-loving teenager is mostly a false one. In fact, teens are often tormented by freedom. A middle school student who was planning to take her new hairstyle to school aptly called this choice "the big dare." In doing so, she testified to a truth parents should appreciate: *asserting adolescent freedom can often be an act of courage.* What one wants to do often must contend with one not wanting to do it as well.

Ambivalence is the motivational conflict between desiring and not desiring to make a given choice at the same time, or the perceptual conflict of seeing some idea or life experience in both favorable and unfavorable terms. Ambivalence can feel conflicting and confusing, making deciding seem impossible: "Unless it feels absolutely sure, I can't decide." Parents might suggest, "So many decisions in life are mixed or uncertain; if it doesn't work out as planned, then there will be other choices that can be made."

Honestly spoken, ambivalence can sound like this: "In some ways I really don't want what I want;" "In some ways I agree with what's going on with my friends, but in other ways I don't;" "In some ways I wish my parents would stop telling me what to do, but in other ways I don't want them to stop." Ambivalence is contradictory in all these ways.

Ambivalence in Adolescence

Growing up, sometimes ambivalence can be a stumbling block. For example, at the end of late adolescence (ages fifteen to eighteen), the high school senior can feel more torn about staying home or leaving home after graduation. They feel mixed, caught between contending desires to hold on to the security of what's familiar and wanting to take the next step and moving out into the larger world: "I want to try out, but it's scary to do." So they want to go to college, but they have a hard time making themselves complete the application. When a young person stalls, rather than get impatient, parents can nudge the application process along: "We'll keep you company tonight for an hour while you push the project through."

Or, in early adolescence (ages nine to thirteen), youthful ambivalence can make it easy to send mixed messages to parents about what is wanted: "Don't tell me again!" "You never remind me!" "Let me alone!" "You never include me!" "I can do it!" "You never help me!"

Parents wonder, which way does the young person want it? The answer is both ways for a while, because growing up requires giving up some childhood dependencies and so can be a source of painful loss. Now, life experience feels like it is becoming more mixed because it is—and not just with their parents.

For the younger adolescent, growing freedom with friends increasingly feels like an iffy proposition, a mix of reward and risk—for example, "If I choose to go, I might not have a good time." "If I join in, I might get hurt." "If I refuse, I might be rejected." "If I question, I might get teased." "If I shut up, I might be trapped." "If I lie, I might get caught." "If I try, I might fail."

Growing up, life just gets more challenging, never less. Everything becomes more of a trade-off. The high school senior was correct: "It was simpler being a child!" Yes, it was.

For the older adolescent, ambivalence about freedom can increase with growing independence as major choices have more influence over one's direction in life. Consider a few unsettling effects:

- **Ambivalence can confuse one's view.** "It's harder to be clear."
- **Ambivalence can cause indecision.** "I don't know which to choose."
- **Ambivalence can take problem-solving.** "It's tough to figure out."
- **Ambivalence can be overloading.** "There's so much to think about."
- **Ambivalence can be disheartening.** "Either way has problems."
- **Ambivalence can feel disorganizing.** "I keep changing my mind."
- **Ambivalence can resist commitment.** "I can't be absolutely sure."
- **Ambivalence can focus on imperfection.** "I can lose some either way."
- **Ambivalence can create anxiety.** "I worry I won't choose for the best."

Emblematic of ambivalence is adolescent indecision in the face of growing complexity. Parents need to be patient when their teenager is having a hard time making up her or his mind. An honorable struggle over freedom of choice is underway: "I'd like to try a part-time job for the money, but I'll lose a lot of social time with friends if I do."

Sometimes ambivalence can be disabling: "I don't know what to do. Those last years, we had a great high school romance, but now we're going off to different colleges. Should we try to keep it together long distance or just let each other go? If we do, suppose we never find another person as good?" Deciding to stay together or separate can feel confounding as indecision bred of ambivalence rules. The freedom challenge of ambivalence is deciding when there is no clear or unmixed easy answer either way.

Growing Ambivalence

In general, there is more ambivalence between teenager and parent than there was between child and parent. Now, adolescent detachment and differentiation from childhood and family are straining their old relationship. In the process of coping with more distance, disagreements, and differences, they don't always match and get on as easily and comfortably as they did during the childhood years. For example, they can find themselves more ill at ease, frustrated, and impatient with each other and can feel less easily connected than they used to be.

Where the parent/child relationship was more idealized ("You're perfectly wonderful!"), the parent/adolescent relationship becomes more mixed ("You're harder to be with"). Love between them doesn't change, but the ease of getting along often does, as the relationship can feel more awkward and abrasive. Thus, it helps if parent and adolescent can develop more tolerance for ambivalence toward each other. For sure, do not give into momentary frustration and declare, "You're not as great to live with as you used to be."

Adolescent ambivalence about freedom is not to be discouraged or stopped; it is to be accepted and utilized. Often, it allows a young person to adequately consider life's complexity when confronting hard decisions they must bravely make. So many major decisions in life are mixed.

Four Freedoms of Adolescent Growth

Observing young people in their adolescent passage, it seems to me that there is a progression through four developmental freedoms as they grow, each one more complicated and more challenging than the last. Describing the accumulating power of these four freedoms is the business of this book. Briefly, the focus of freedom changes as adolescents grow in four developmental ways.

1. **Freedom from rejection of childhood** begins in late elementary school around ages nine through thirteen. Pushing away from their old definition, in words and actions the young person says, "I'm not a little child anymore!" Now early adolescence begins with the young person refusing to act or be treated in former childlike ways. For example, old childhood pastimes with parents are given up. The cost of this freedom is *loss*.

2. **Freedom with association with peers** becomes more important in middle school, around ages thirteen though fifteen. Joining a culture of companions, in words and actions, the young person says, "Peers matter most!" Now mid-adolescence starts by forming a family of friends. For example, now there are more social pressures to keep up, fit in, and belong. The cost of this freedom is *conformity*.

3. **Freedom for older experimentation** becomes more common in high school, around ages fifteen through eighteen. Impelled by curiosity and pressured by peers, in words and actions the young person says, "I'm ready to act more grown up!" Now late adolescence begins by older risk-taking. For example, more dangerous adult experiences are tried. The cost of this freedom is risking *danger*.

4. Freedom to claim emancipation increases in the college-age years, around ages eighteen through twenty-three. Letting go of an old reliance on their parents, in words and actions the young person says, "It's time for me to run my own life!" Now trial independence begins by claiming personal agency and authority. For example, direction for oneself is assumed. The cost of this freedom is *responsibility*.

The Parental Adjustment

With the growth of each freedom, parents usually have some catching up to do because the terms of the adolescent relationship with them can significantly change, creating some hardship, but also some positive possibility.

With *freedom from rejection of childhood*, parents can feel more *disfavored*: "At the moment, we're less fun to play with." However, parents can refuse to take this rejection personally: "His dissatisfaction with us is really with how he used to be with us and with himself." Parents can keep perspective and give understanding.

With *freedom with association with peers*, parents can feel more socially *marginalized*: "At the moment, she mostly wants time with friends." However, parents can continue to initiate positive companionship with their daughter, while welcoming valued peers into the family circle: "We're glad you brought them over." Parents can still provide good company while supporting the importance of friends.

With *freedom for advanced experimentation*, parents can feel more *worried*: "Suppose he dares the dangerous and gets hurt?" However, parents can be reliable informants about significant risk-taking— what to watch out for and how to act safely: "Here's something you might want to consider." Parents can provide the protection of preparation and prediction.

With *freedom to claim emancipation*, parents can feel *demoted* in importance: "We're not socially central anymore!" However, parents still matter—as a source of unwavering love, as cheerleaders who encourage, and as mentors who can share lessons from personal life when asked: "We can tell you what we learned the hard way from trying that, if you'd like to know." Sharing parental experience can provide a wealth of real-world education.

So with every opportunity that each of these four freedoms brings, there are new challenges as well. That's how life is. Thus, the adventure of adolescence ordains

- **Rejection**—to grow up, you must let go acting like a child.
- **Association**—to grow up, you must rely on peer companionship.
- **Experimentation**—to grow up, you must try experiences that older people do.
- **Emancipation**—to grow up, you must forsake depending on parental care.

There really is no other way. To varying degrees, at varying times, an adolescent is a rebel with a cause, and the name of that cause is freedom to grow.

Part One

• • •

Freedom from Rejection of Childhood

The Late Elementary School Years

"Quit babying and bossing me!"

Let the separation from childhood begin!

The entry into adolescence that can start in late elementary school can feel less comfortable than childhood. Consider it this way.

"Of course I still love my parents, but I have more to complain about because they're harder to live with now, not mostly fun like they used to be, making objections and demands when I just want to be left alone, free to do what I'm doing, promising to do what they want later and they get angry when I don't, more arguing with them when they're being unfair by saying 'no,' arguing, which they call 'talking back' so just do as I'm told, and now it's harder to find good times we used to have, too old for all that hugging now which feels embarrassing, worse in public, and a lot of fun stuff together no longer is, because I'm grown beyond that now, I don't know why, saying goodbye to those good times, missing how things used to be, not always knowing what to do instead, more often bored and ready for

doing something different, not knowing exactly what, so want-
ing better company than parents, ready to dare what's different,
some that parents won't approve and better not be told, even
lying, sometimes ignoring rules and limits, seeing what can be
gotten away with, creating worry about being caught, caring
less about school grades, letting them slide, maybe skipping
homework for what feels better to do, wanting just getting by to
be good enough, so parents get on my case since I'm forgetting
more, because there's too much to remember, plus it's harder to
pay attention with all that's going on, more messy so it's easier
to lose things, and they say I leave stuff laying everywhere,
but if they'd look the other way and let me keep my room door
closed and just stayed out they wouldn't have to mind, and so
with more annoyance and less fun time together, that's where
we are!"

Well, maybe that's an exaggeration, but on some days not so much.

Freedom from rejection of childhood terms commonly starts in late elementary school around ages nine through thirteen, what I have called "early adolescence." In words and actions the young person expresses discontent: "I don't want to be defined and treated as just a little child anymore!"

As for parents, they may notice some unwelcome changes: "He agrees and listens less and ignores and argues more." And now begins more active and passive resistance to parents' authority—actively questioning and disagreeing with what they want ("Just tell me why?") and passively ignoring and delaying what they ask for ("I said I'd do it later!"). To some degree, the young adolescent rebels out of childhood by opposing traditional adult restraints and demands that limit individual freedom. Best for parents not to take this resistance personally; it is not about them but needing to shed some of the kid way they used to be.

It is self-dissatisfaction that drives this desire for developmental change: "Been there, done that" seems to be the rejection taking place. This creates two problems: letting go what's valued and figuring out what will matter now instead. It can feel easier to reject something old, to rebel out of childhood, than to create something new to care about, to find and try positive possibilities. The early adolescent must do both. *Now begins the awkward and liberating separation from childhood* when the girl or boy wants some different definition but doesn't yet know exactly what, all of which parents find unfamiliar: "He's more at loose ends than he used to be."

The Onset of Adolescence

While it may be delayed (as often can happen with a closely attached only child), there's no getting around it: *adolescence begins with loss.* The letting go of childhood starts the long redefining process of detaching for more functional independence and differentiating for more fitting individuality. In doing so, some strain is put on the old relationship to parents who more frequently wonder about where to begin letting go and where to still hold on: "How much do we still decide how she dresses, and how much do we leave up to her?"

For the young adolescent, loss can be experienced as not knowing how to occupy oneself now, so she or he is more frequently restless and bored: "There's nothing to do!" As for the parental loss, it can be experienced as not knowing just who they are dealing with now, more frequently feeling awkward and out of familiar step with their changing child: "The old joking around often isn't fun or funny with him anymore."

To some degree, there is also a parental fall from childhood grace: "It used to be we could do little wrong; now it seems we can do less right!" Parents are removed from their ideal-ized standing in the child's eyes and are cut down to imperfect size. This alteration is a necessary loss because it also gives the changing child permission to be less perfect: "If I'm harder to get along with, so are you!" As the early adolescent falls from childhood grace in parental eyes, parents become less idealized too. Now each has more complaints about the other than before.

Adolescent Discontent

The message communicating that adolescence has begun can be a contrary and critical one when the child rebels out of childhood by rejecting and opposing some old terms of treat-ment and definition. Now there can be a spike in complaints: "Why do I need a bedtime anymore?" Now the allure of more nighttime freedom begins to call. Explains the parent, "Because the later you stay up, the harder you are to wake up in the morn-ing." And then some words are said in support of getting ade-quate rest.

Parents will never have this daughter or son as a little child anymore. Both parent and young adolescent will fondly remem-ber how life between them, that precious mutual entrancement relationship, often used to be. However, this loss can be harder on parents. Although the young person can miss what is given up, she looks forward to older changes that come next. Parents, however, can feel bereft of the old easy connection that is lost: "We miss the good old days with him!"

Yet the young person has moments of missing something precious too. Rejecting childhood toys and pastimes, old pleasurable ways of being with parents, all for the sake of acting older, he or she can never go back to that simpler, sheltered, and secure world of childhood again. The price of growing up is giving up—what every early adolescent has to pay: "I miss how we were, but I want something more!"

Growth Pressure

Then there is pressure to stop acting like a child.. Socially, the child can feel penalized by peers for not acting and appearing older. One can get teased for acting and looking childlike. In addition, now parents can become unintentionally complicit in this rejection of childhood by welcoming that sought-after compliment from their adult friends: "Your child is so grown up!"

Adults can socially reward speed of growth. Looking and acting older can not only confer standing with peers, it can also yield compliments to parents from other adults: "Your child looks so old!" This can get pretty complicated. Within is a competitive community culture, it seems like the child who develops the fastest wins the most standing, with parents socially benefiting accordingly: "You must be so proud to have someone who looks and acts so mature!" The cultural message for adolescents seems to be: "Get over being a child and be done with it as soon as you can." What rate of growth through childhood do parents want to encourage and allow is one question. Another is what's the hurry?

Sometimes growing up quickly through childhood is more functionally related: "In our family with so many children, you didn't play around. You started contributing work very young, with the older taking some care of the younger at an early age—that was the family rule."

The Gift of Loss

While giving up the beloved familiarities of childhood can feel costly to the adolescent, the other side of loss is freedom—freedom from the old child definition, and freedom for older, new possibilities: "I never thought of trying this before!" And now parents can behold some exciting changes: a nonreading child may discover the company of books, a physically inactive child may become more athletic, an inward child may get into performing, or a solitary child may change into a social joiner. For many children, the onset of adolescence energizes and opens up positive possibilities.

However, often some unwelcome family price must be paid. For example, when adolescence changes the child who becomes less immediately compliant, it can change the parent in response, who becomes more prone to nagging about delay. As the adolescent becomes more resistant, the parent becomes more insistent. So now there is more disagreement about what needs to be done, sometimes making it harder to get along.

The relationship can frequently become more abrasive, and this is functional as it gradually starts the developmental process of wearing down the dependence between them—the young person pushing for more letting go, parents deciding on when and when not to keep holding on.

Through this process of opposition and separation, more differences grow between them; they don't fit together as easily. Interests start diverging, and wants can increasingly conflict. Now it can be harder to hang out, as some endearing companionship is lost: "My child doesn't want to play this with me anymore!" Just as the parent must give up having their daughter or son as a play companion, the young person can't recapture the old easy childhood intimacy with parents: "They're not so much fun to be with now."

Add to this change the emerging cultural influence of peers and popular entertainment. Now, more cultural separation between parent and teenager begins, no matter how close they remain. Offline and online play calls to the adolescent in compelling, worldly, influential ways that can seem strange to parents who are used to more traditional fare: "We can't understand how she likes doing that and wanting to be like that." And now the generational divide begins growing between them.

Treating Differentness

With the rejection of childhood, negative and positive choices create contrast from how things used to be, resulting in separation from childhood and parents for precious room to grow. The loving trick for parents is to accept the rejection without taking it personally. The young person is not rejecting *them*, only much of the conduct and treatment that went with being a child. Parents have to decide what to let go of that the growing child feels ready to cast aside. At the same time, they often have to restate requirements that they continue to hold: "Even though you're getting older, remember that following household rules, giving family help, and keeping us adequately informed remain what we expect of you."

In general, don't criticize the brave child for daring this developmental change: "You used to be such a great kid. What happened to you?" Rather than reject the rejection of childhood and pull away, be grateful for the period of mutual entrancement that was given. A precious period of physical and emotional closeness with parents is ending, and now the time for *growing separation,* which is what adolescence is about, begins.

Helping parents grieve this loss, honoring their honest pain, I try to help them understand that, wonderful as childhood was, it can't compare to the adolescent coming-of-age passage that is underway. Now parents get to witness and play a supportive part in an amazing transformation: seeing their little girl grow into a young woman and their little boy into a young man.

What is more magical than this?

Chapter Five

Rejection and Identity

● ● ●

"I'm not like I was anymore."

Because growing up requires giving up, adolescence is often an act of courage. To change, one must dare to let go of the fond familiar and brave the challenging unknown. To create more freedom, some old definitions must be forsaken, with this loss creating opportunity for new development to grow.

In the process, the old relationship with parents is affected. As the young person pulls away and pushes against familiar limits and demands, the relationship with parents can become more strained, creating an adjustment not always to either of their liking.

As adolescence proceeds along the two paths of growth mentioned earlier—detachment and differentiation from childhood and parents—there is more discord and more diversity to manage in the relationship.

- **Detaching from childhood and parents** to assert independence creates more conflicts over freedom of action, with

complaint and protest sometimes sounding like "stop controlling everything I do!"

• **Differentiating from childhood and parents** to express individuality creates more contrasts in personal expression, with
complaint and protest sometimes sounding like "quit telling
me how to be!"

On both counts, parents can feel less compatible with their more
unfamiliar adolescent, who can also feel less compatible with them.
Compared to the child who prized the harmony and similarity of
parental company, now the young person can find parents more often
in the way and out of touch. Thus for some parents, the onset of
adolescence (starting around ages nine to thirteen) can be dispiriting when their traditional companionship with the child undergoes
some degree of alteration.

A parental account of this change might sound like this: "We used
to have such a great relationship, but she's become so irritated by me
now. In little ways I'm hard for her to stand. That's when she'll have
something critical to say. Like this morning, I'm spreading butter on
my toast—I use the back of a spoon—and she asks, 'Mom, why do
you have to be the way you are?' Grumpy with herself, she takes it
out on me! At worst I feel treated like an enemy! Is she going to grow
up disliking her parent? I used to be appreciated, but now I'm more
frequently blamed! What changed my child?"

The Adjustment

My favorite description of this loss of familiarity came to me years
ago from a mom explaining her anguish at seeing adolescence change
the cozy old relationship with her beloved son. To get me to understand her upset, she asked, "Well, how would you like it if you woke

up one day to find that your devoted dog had turned into a distant cat?"

That caught my attention. We spent a few minutes educating my understanding about the unwelcome alteration in her son. In summary, she found the old child/dog to be mostly friendly, affectionate, compliant, close, playful, pleasing, communicative, caring, and warm; but now she was often dealing with an adolescent/cat—sometimes more aloof, moody, contrary, insensitive, prickly, irritable, private, unsociable, and cool. "This isn't the child I signed up for anymore!"

Of course, the love between her and her son had not changed, but at times the relationship had become more challenging to manage. When the young person rejects old child definitions, parents must adjust to the change. At times it can feel like there is now less to like and feeling less liked, more distance and less closeness, less compatibility and more awkwardness, less harmony and more disagreement. You can appreciate this doting parent's complaint: "We were such good company, and now it's harder to enjoy time together! Who changed my child?"

Her question had a piece of the truth because at times the transformation into adolescence can be quite dramatic, the parent unprepared for normal rejections of childhood that often occur.

Name Changes

Rejection of the old familiar child identity and treatment takes many forms. As younger is rejected, older can be requested. For example, wanting to be seen and treated differently than as a child, the young adolescent occasionally demands a name change to mark the difference that growing older brings. A fuller name can feel more fitting and freeing than a shorter, diminutive name: "Don't call me

Susie, call me Susan!" "Don't call me Richie, call me Richard!" "What's the difference? Lindy was my baby name; call me Melinda!" Formal can feel older than familiar.

Sometimes this change rejects an old affectionate name that parents loved to use but that now feels ill-fitting, even embarrassing to the young person, particularly when around peers: "Don't call me that!" Rejection of an old pet name can feel liberating: "I'm not your little Cookie anymore!" Other adolescents who hear the name might start some good-natured but embarrassing teasing from friends: "Hey, Cookie, what's happening?"

Then there are more common behavior changes as early adolescent rejection leads to redefinition, causing some lessening of what parents liked about the child, changes that parents can find unwelcome to deal with now.

Unwelcome Rejections

None of the normal "lessening" that follows mean parents undergo any loss of love or loving. *They do not.* However, to varying degrees the young person is going to reject some child ways to create more separation in ways that can be more challenging for parents. For example, compared to younger times, an early adolescent may act

- Less compliant and more *unwilling*: "Do I have to?"
- Less cooperative and more *resistant*: "I don't want to!"
- Less affectionate and more *standoffish*: "Don't hug me!"
- Less agreeable and more *argumentative*: "Why should I?"
- Less social and more *unfriendly*: "Leave me alone!"
- Less asking and more *demanding*: "Just let me!"
- Less interested and more *bored*: "There's nothing to do!"
- Less cheerful and more *moody*: "I'm grumpy!"

- Less admiring and more *critical*: "You're no fun!"
- Less social and more *separate*: "I don't want to go!"
- Less communicative and more *private*: "Don't ask me!"
- Less helpful and more *uncooperative*: "I'm too tired!"
- Less retentive and more *forgetful*: "I can't remember!"
- Less prompt and more *delaying*: "I'll do it later!"
- Less orderly and more *disorganized*: "I can't find it!"
- Less focused and more *distracted*: "I wasn't paying attention!"

To some degree, such changes and many others can add up to losing a lot of familiar characteristics for parents who, missing what they loved, may turn grief into grievance against the young person: "She used to be such a great kid!"

If a parent criticizes and blames the girl or boy for normal alterations that come with entering adolescence—changes that the adolescent is responsible for managing but is not at fault for creating—damage can be done. Now a young person, who to some degree is already coping with childhood losses of her or his own, can feel deprived of parental acceptance and support at a very vulnerable time: "They don't like me like they did!"

Remember that how parents respond is like a powerful mirror in which the girl or boy sees a trusted reflection of themselves. At a disenchanted age, the adolescent in response to parental criticism may proudly declare, "I don't care what you think!" This is a lie. Like the child he was, the young adolescent still wants to shine in his parents' eyes. The youth still takes his own measure partly by the measure his parents take of him. And at a developmental time when so much painful self-rejection of childhood identity is going on, the teenager doesn't need any more from his parents.

Resenting Rejection

Parents who were closely attached to childhood companionship and sharing can sometimes take early adolescent rejection of familiarity personally: "My considerate young daughter has turned into such a self-centered teenager. She doesn't make any effort with us anymore. I used to love her company, but now I'm more inclined to leave her to herself!" *Resenting the rejection of childhood can inflict injury, encourage estrangement, and risk the young person feeling that she or he has been abandoned by parental love*: "They loved me better when I was younger."

How sad for all concerned when parental resentment has its angry way, and how self-defeating such a response can be. To better cope with the loss of one's daughter's or son's beloved childhood time, honor feelings of grief but don't indulge in grievance. It embitters the holder and alienates the relationship. Shun resentment. Better to attend to that common piece of adolescent advice in defense of personal change: "Get used to it!"

A parental response that might work best is one that values the past and is excited about the future. Maybe it could sound something like, "I just want you to know that I loved our cozy childhood time together and am forever grateful that we had it. Now I look forward to what comes next, watching you pull away to become your own independent and individual person, and being a loving and supportive part of your growing up."

It works better if parents can adjust their expectations to fit a growing reality, lovingly providing a firm family structure of responsible rules for their adolescent to operate within, and maintaining caring communication while the young person starts redefining in older ways.

A More Assertive Age

Adolescence is a more assertive age as the young person starts to grow up partly by becoming more *resistant* and *insistent* on their own behalf. Adolescence is a gathering of power this way, as beginning in late elementary or early middle school, the young person starts detaching for more independence and differentiating for more individuality. Over the next ten to twelve years, this coming-of-age will transform a parent-directed child into a self-directed young adult.

At the outset, parents can notice a telling change as the adolescent starts becoming increasingly assertive on their own behalf.

Parents encounter growing assertiveness in their child in two ways. They experience more *resistance* ("I won't!" "Why must I?") and more *insistence* ("I want!" "Why can't I?"). In each case, assertive resistance and assertive insistence express freedom's call. More running room is desired.

Both these changes put pressure on parents when they are standing by rules and requirements and when they are deliberating provision and permission. More self-determined than a child, the adolescent is becoming more strong-willed. Now a healthy young person feels impelled to push for more freedom to grow, while healthy parents feel obliged to restrain that push within the interests of safety and responsibility. And this healthy conflict of interests unfolds over the course of adolescence.

Growing Differences

More growing disagreement is not evidence of an adolescent and parents not getting along; it is a functional part of *how* they now must get along as they continually broker emerging differences that redefine their changing relationship: "Last year you said I couldn't wear makeup, but this year that's what all my friends are allowed to do." "Last year you drove me around, but this year I'm old enough to bus myself downtown!"

On the parent side, new freedoms in the form of more responsibilities are also being taught and given in recognition of increased capacity for self-care: "It's time you helped us and yourself in more grown-up ways." And now parents begin to offload some services they used to provide the child: "From now on, once a week you strip your bed, collect your dirty clothes, wash and dry the lot, make your bed, and put what's clean away." And if the young adolescent complains, they reply, "You wanted us to let you do more. Well, this is part of how we will."

Resistance

Resistance is about *freedom to oppose*. One formula for discord in human relationships is a cooperative one: *resistance + resistance = conflict*. It takes both parties agreeing to disagree over some issue to create a conflict. Thus, by contesting some difference in wants by mutually opposing it and attacking each other's position, both parties can create a quarrel. For resolution, they have to decide whether both want to stick to their guns to win the encounter by battling it out, whether one or the other is willing to concede, or whether they want to dialogue to find compromise both can support.

Conflict can drive people apart or bring them together. Because there tends to be more parental disagreement with an assertive teenager, the process of talking out differences and coming to some joint agreement tends to work better than fighting out differences and one side winning. Plus, practicing this resolution process can have a formative influence in the young person's later relationships: "I learned with my parents how disagreement is just a time to discuss and work things out."

Argument

For some parents, argument from a teenager is treated as disrespectful of their authority: "Don't you talk back to me; just do what you're told!" However, such parents are often misguided. Resistant argument is respectful because it engages with the parent by questioning their directive, expressing objection, and wanting to talk about it. *True disrespect is when the teenager simply ignores and tunes out whatever parental authority has to say.*

For perspective, parents who want no argument with their adolescent might remember this: if they think having an argumentative adolescent is hard to bear, let them try having a silent teenager who tells them almost nothing at all: "We have no clue to what he's thinking, feeling, or doing because he never says!" Now they perceive they have a *mystery child*: impossible to know.

A mystery child can leave a lot to parental imagination when parents misread the young person in their attempt to figure out what is happening. They might project their worst fears on their daughter's silence: "She's probably secretly disappointed about what we gave her for her birthday. That's why she's acting down." No, she's just tired from staying up so late after her parents told her to go to sleep. But how are they to know when they haven't been told?

Set the conditions for argument. The teenager is speaking up for herself and communicating disagreement, a skill that will serve her well in other relationships and in life to come. So now parents can model and talk about the healthy conduct of disagreement: "I don't call you names in anger, and I don't want you doing that to me. Using hurtful words with me or my doing so with you doesn't help us work out disagreement and learn to get along."

Also, appreciate this trade-off. Sometimes when parents take a hard stand with their insistent teenager who is angrily opposed to being refused, actively listening to all the disappointed teen's objections and frustrations can help with the adjustment: "I really disagreed with their decision but went along with it because at least I got to have all my say." Insistence can have a very hard time accepting denial; however, being given a full hearing can allow the young person to let this disagreement go.

Insistence

More outspoken and stubborn about it, more self-dedicated, more determined to explore and experiment with life, more influenced by what friends are doing or want to do, more willing to face parental disapproval, more dedicated to pursuing what personally matters: insistence seeks freedom on these counts and others. Just as resistance was about freedom to oppose, insistence is about freedom to experience. *Insistence + pursuit = ambition.*

Insistence is often investment. What the teenager wants is tied to expectations for enjoyment or because of commitments made: "If you don't let me, I'll be the only one of my friends who can't go!" Adolescent insistence is often about something that really matters to them, so denial can create significant loss. This is all the more reason for parents to listen to what their denial has cost: "I have to have that outfit to look okay!"

Insistence also goes hand in hand with ambition, the awakening desire to make something of or to get something for oneself, more so than is currently the case: "I want to see if I can!" Adolescence awakens many dreams because now the world is filled with possibilities formerly reserved to older people. However, ambition without insistence gains little traction. Insistence can take self-discipline to sustain, so where parents see their teenager investing continual effort in life, they can tell what truly matters at the time: "He spends long hours working out." "She won't stop rehearsing until she gets it right."

In Praise of Assertion

Developmentally, the twin powers of adolescent assertion—resistance and insistence—begin the process of exercising more influence over one's life, finally maturing into assuming full *young-adult agency* when growing up is done: "At last, how I am and what I do is up to me!"

Parents might want to appreciate both powers of assertion—developing strengths of resistance and insistence in their adolescent that are of lasting value in many ways. For example, resistance won't be mistreated, and insistence won't quit; resistance will protect, and insistence will pursue; resistance withstands temptation, and insistence sticks to principle; resistance opposes what is wrong, and insistence works for what is right. *Raising an assertive adolescent can be wise.*

When these adolescent powers of assertion contest their authority, parents in their aggravation need to be sure that they don't crush these expressions of opposition and determination. One parent summed up admiration of his older adolescent's assertion this way: "Based on how she was in the family, watch out, world. That's all I can say! As her dad I can testify, nobody's going to push her around or stand in her way!"

Liking Your Adolescent

"Adolescence is the time when you and your child still love each other as always but often don't like each other as much." So I was told on good parental authority.

While the early years were often filled with parents and child taking pleasure in each other's company, like a mutual appreciation society, the push against and pull away of adolescence is often more wearing on their relationship as growing separation and differentiation come between them. Now, at times, each can find the other harder to live with.

This perception is mutual—and it needs to be because for the adolescent to let her or his "bad " (more resistant) side out, parents have to be taken down from the pedestal of perfection on which the child had them placed. *If I'm not as good as I was, you're not as great as you were*, seems to be how the young person is thinking. *If you have more to criticize about me now, I have more to criticize about you.* Some traditional liking of each other's behaviors has been lost on both sides.

It's a mutually painful part of separation: come adolescence, parent and child are both critically downsized in each other's eyes. No teenager can afford to have a perfect parent, any more than any adolescent can afford to be a parent's perfect child. Each must lose some idealized luster in the other's eyes. Some loss of childhood popularity often occurs on both sides.

Less Alike and Liking

For the parents, gone is the adoring and adorable little child whose tag-along, play-together company they miss. For the adolescent, gone are the perfectly wonderful parents and the fun-loving company they used to be. For both parent and changing child, adolescence begins with some loss of mutual enjoyment, and *liking* is its name. Come adolescence, some lessening of familiar liking on both sides of the relationship can occur.

Although it can feel easy to blame each other for this disaffection, the real culprit is growth. Now, three developmental engines—separation, contrast , and opposition—drive the adolescent transformation toward more independence and individuality. Contention can occur more frequently: "You haven't done what I asked!" collides with, "I said I would—in a while!"

Increased abrasion from normal differences starts wearing down the familiar connection between them, gradually pushing them more apart from each other. This is what the coming-of-age passage is meant to accomplish—partly through developing more reliance, partly by expressing more resistance, and partly by assuming more responsibility.

Love Is Not Enough

To some parents, this partial loss of liking from loss of familiarity seems like no big deal as long as lasting love remains strong because loving surely counts more than liking. Yes and no. If you could only have one, certainly love would be best choice. However, never underestimate the power of parental liking. Consider it this way.

The *power of parental love* is nurturing *attachment* on which trust in the lasting power of this unconditional commitment depends: "I know my parents have always loved me and always will." We are talking about a trusting foundation here: "Looking back, even during the hard times between myself and my parents, what kept me going was the certainty that I was loved."

The *power of parental liking* is providing *affirmation* of strengths on which much constant *self-esteem* depends. Self-esteem is two concepts combined into one: how one *defines* oneself and how one *evaluates* oneself. *Building a strong self-esteem requires defining oneself broadly and evaluating oneself kindly*: "There's a lot I like to do, and I like who and how I am."

Parents have some formative responsibility here. When parents help the young person find what he likes doing, and when they continually communicate what they appreciate about him, parental liking can encourage youthful self-esteem.

Criticism and Self-Dislike

Critical parents can engender self-critical children when the young person learns never to be satisfied with how they are and what they do: "I was taught that I can always be a better person than I am and should never be satisfied."

Young adolescents can dislike themselves more than they did as children on two counts. First, when they cast off childhood interests, they can have less they like to do, opening the door to more boredom. And second, when they evaluate how they're growing older, compared with peers, they can find themselves lacking and lagging, opening the door to more self-criticism. Beset by both dislikes, the young person might declare, "I have nothing to do! I don't like how I am!"

It is very common when young people *separate from childhood* and start adolescence (around ages nine to thirteen) for them to have fewer grounds for liking themselves. This is a time for parents to help with an *emotional reset*: "Let us help you find some activities you might enjoy trying, and we want to tell you all the parts of you that we prize."

While some adolescents are gifted with old interests and skills from childhood, like a beloved sport or musical expression that they want to continue to grow, many young people are not. For these, it takes exploration to replace old enjoyments and supports, and until these replacements are found, a young person can feel beset by self-dislike and dissatisfaction.

Liking and Love

Because love amplifies the importance of the loved one's power of liking—of approval and disapproval—criticism from a loved one can hurt the most. The young person can have concerns that wrongful actions may harm the relationship, even fear that loss of parental liking may endanger parental love. "My parents don't like how I've changed!"

Thus, sometimes in response to an infraction of a significant rule, the anxious offender who wonders if they've really torn the relationship with parents now may require parental reassurance. Sensing this insecurity, parents explain, "Just because we don't like how you acted on this occasion doesn't mean we don't love who you are as much as ever."

Examples of Active Liking

So how might an adolescent experience *active parental liking*? Consider some common examples of what adolescents may say to express this experience:

- "You enjoy my company."
- "You welcome my friends."
- "You compliment my efforts."
- "You support my goals."
- "You listen with attention."

- "You understand my changes."
- "You respect my needs."
- "You appreciate my interests."
- "You value my opinion."
- "You laugh at my humor."
- "You're glad to see me."

While parents should be steadfast in loving their young adolescent, they should also be constant in actively expressing their liking too, particularly the growing differences from the child who was and from how parents are: "We appreciate how you are growing yourself up!"

Chapter Six

Rejection and Adequacy

● ● ●

"I don't measure up!"

During late elementary school and into middle school, young people can have more emotional downs than in younger years, becoming moodier to live with for themselves and for family as well. A common complaint seems to be feeling *inadequate*, self-rejecting for *not being good enough* in who they are, how they do, how they look, and how they wish they were. What's going on?

Looking around at media portrayals and popular peers, adolescence now becomes a more comparative (not feeling as ideal as) and competitive (not feeling keeping up with) age. It's easy to feel inadequate and insufficient on both counts: "Sometimes I think my twelve-year-old has an inferiority complex! He's down on us because he's down on himself. We tell him to lighten up. But he tells us to leave him alone because we just don't understand!"

Usually not this extreme, she or he is still beset by more self-criticism, insecurity, and doubts, particularly when getting ready for school, dreading what peers at school will see and say. This is all the more reason to keep a criticism-free household because the young teenager is so vulnerable to put-downs. "I don't care what you think of me!" the young person defiantly declares, but the reality is that she or he cares too much to let that caring show. *What's going on?* wonder concerned parents.

Adolescent Change

Often, the outset of adolescence is the answer. Starting with the separation from childhood (around ages nine to thirteen), the coming-of-age passage is now underway. One's world of experience is becoming altered—from being centered on family to being focused on friends, from recreational play to working at acting more grown-up.

As the young person starts changing physical appearance, striving to act older, and maintaining social membership with peers, contentment becomes more challenging. On harder days, comparing oneself to others can feel like one just can't compete, keep up, catch up, fit in, be accepted, or socially belong: *I'm such a loser!*

Measuring oneself against prominent peers and popular images, engaging in self-criticism from answers to comparison questions can lead to torment. For example, what is enough confidence, ability, smartness, achievement, looks, shapeliness, size, friendship, fashion, popularity, possessions, happiness, knowledge, experience, or success? It's easy to feel discontent: *I wish I were like that!*

"How to be and how not to be?" is the troubling early-adolescent question. And when a deficiency is felt, a lot of unhappiness can follow: *I don't like how I am!* No wonder feelings of inadequacy and insufficiency can bedevil the early and mid-adolescent years. Enter the *three reflection miseries.*

- No wonder *media misery* comes from viewing idealized young icons: *I'll never get to look as good as that!*
- No wonder *mirror misery* comes when just getting ready for school can be a challenge: *I just get to see how I wish I wasn't!*
- No wonder *meanness misery* from peer teasing and other aggression hurts so much: *Others don't like me, and I don't either!*

Taking these experiences personally, it's easy to feel like a misfit, an oddball, a reject, a loser, a failure: *I'll never grow into the person I'd like to be!* Parents to the rescue! Hearing any self-denigrating comments, they can empathize with unhappy feelings, positively disagree by offering honest affirmations, and suggest that hard times are the best times to treat themselves well: "What about doing something fun?"

Parenting Is Affected

Increasing feelings of deficiency may be expressed through irritability at home. More critical of themselves, they can be more critical of parents who complain, "She's become so negative to live with!"

However, before taking this behavior personally by getting offended, parents are usually better served by asking the young person some empathetic questions: "Has this been a hard day?" "Are you having a down time, and would talking about it help?" "Do you need some alone time to feel better?" "Is there anything we can do that would lift your spirits?"

But suppose the young teenager feels stuck: "Stop blaming me for being down! I can't help it! I can't change how I feel!" When discouragement feels emotionally overwhelming, finding other options can be hard. However, parents can help.

For many teenagers, striving for ideals can have a lot of unhappiness to answer for. Why?

The developmental transformation called "adolescence" can be a painfully self-evaluative time. It is an impressionable age as young people feel compelled to redefine their identity on many levels. Socially, for example, comparisons are constantly made with popular peers and media images that embody *ideals* for growing up that feel very hard to meet. In consequence, a young person can end up falling short in her or his own eyes, feeling badly on that account: "I'll never measure up!"

Common pillars of self-esteem and sources of social approval have to do with appearance, performance, and status: "I'm worth how well I look, how well I do, and how much I'm liked." Thus, ideals of beauty, success, and popularity can seem worth pursuing. The notion is that the more one approximates these ideals, the happier one will become. The problem is that, for those who attain these perceived ideals, maintaining this outcome can prove costly: "Staying popular takes a lot of work!"

Adequacy Conflicts

I believe most teenagers experience some *adequacy conflicts* between the actuality of how one is and the ideal of how one wishes to be. At issue is being "good enough" compared with what is generally promoted as "how best to be." For example, consider those images propagated by the media, entertainment, fashion, diet, and advertising industries depicting the most desirable models of personal appearance to which one can aspire. These portraits of physical ideals can tyrannize a young person's growing self-consciousness. Even knowing that most everyone isn't created this way, there is the sense that at best they should be.

Falling short of such ideals can encourage feelings of inferiority, even shame over not being sufficiently womanly or manly: "I'll never have a body like that!" "I'll never be shapely enough!" "I'll never be built enough!" At worst, "I hate how I look!" With such self-talk, that brutal morning confrontation with one's mirror image can be extremely painful: *This is who I have to take to school today!*

Or there are simply bad days that only illuminate one's imperfections: "I had a bad hair day!" "I had a bad skin day!" "I had a bad friend day!" "I had a bad dress day!" "I had a bad game day!" "I had a bad test day!" There are so many ways for one's day to depart from the ideal. On a very down day, a young person can feel, "I don't like me. Nobody else likes me. I'm such a loser. My life sucks!" Parents can sometimes help resuscitate the young person's view of themselves.

They might explain to their discontented adolescent that subscribing to an ideal is a complicated choice because ideals themselves are complex—appealing to create, inspiring to follow, and difficult to resist—they can be laborious to pursue, hard to meet, and burdensome to bear. The higher one aspires, the more one can fall short of extreme standards that idealism has set: *I really let myself down!*

Is an ideal worth believing in, worth striving for, worth measuring oneself against? I believe the answer is sometimes yes when it motivates effort but often no when failure results in self-punishment. Parents can help their teenager make a merciful separation. "Maybe say to yourself: *Ideally this is what I wish for, but realistically this is what I expect. At best, ordinary and average is how most of us are most of the time, and that is perfectly okay.*"

If your adolescent is disturbed by dissatisfaction for not being perfect or doing perfectly and continually self-critical on that account, you might want to propose an alternative to idealism.

How to forsake the tyranny of ideals? Parents might suggest committing to a more humane objective: prizing one's *individuality*: "Rather than pursue some popular ideal, honor the personal mix of characteristics and capacities you've been given. Then commit to nurture the distinct human being that no one else but you can ever be. Instead of asking, *How can I become like what I admire in others?* ask instead, *How can I develop what is uniquely me?*"

Teaching Self-Management

"You're right: feelings can be very hard to change directly. However, *you don't have to change your feelings to change your feelings.*" Say what? Parents can explain this in the following manner: "Experience is all connected—your feelings, thoughts, and actions all influence each other. For example, if you think *no one* likes you, you may decide to keep to yourself, and can end up feeling lonely on that account. However, if you think *some* people might like you, and if you act socially with others, then you will probably start feeling less alone. So whenever you're in a funk from feeling down you might ask yourself, *What good thoughts and fun activities might make me happy?* and maybe take a break by doing some of those."

Affirmative Parenting

Finally, consider three parenting practices that can counter "not good enough" thinking in a young adolescent.

 • **No criticism allowed.** All criticism sends a "not good enough" message. Best for parents to keep a criticism- and tease-free family, particularly during the discontented and vulnerable early adolescent years. Rather than say, "You're doing it wrong," suggest, "You might try it this way instead."

- **Use nonevaluative correction.** When adolescent misbehavior or misdeeds have occurred, parents can use nonevaluative correction in response. Take issue with choices; don't attack character: "We disagree with the decision you have made. This is why, this is what we need to have happen now, and as always we want to listen to whatever you have to say."

- **Encourage positive appreciation.** Social comparison with others can feel easy to do for young teenagers, so parents can provide this caution: "When you measure yourself by making comparisons to others, you are at risk of ignoring how you are truly beyond compare. Please remember, no one in the world is exactly like you, so prize the special person you are. We'll be happy to help you count the wonderful ways."

Building Confidence

For the young adolescent, confidence can often be hard to achieve. During childhood, the girl or boy may have felt relatively self-assured in the smaller, simpler, and sheltered world of home and family. But with the onset of adolescence (around ages nine to thirteen), with increased social comparison and competition, more developmental insecurity begins. Now, as the teenager separates from childhood and parents to start the daunting coming-of-age passage through the larger world toward young-adult independence—to young womanhood or young manhood at the end—it's hard not to gauge one's progress by the excellence of others.

Growing up keeps introducing more changes and challenges in the teenager's path, creating fresh cause for self-doubt: *I'm not as good! I can't keep up! I won't fit in! I'll never learn! How will I get it done?* Parents may not always appreciate how, when youthful confidence is lacking, adolescence requires acts of courage to proceed: "Some days, just showing up at school can feel brave to do!"

How to help a young person cope with lack of confidence? By way of example, consider the common case of social shyness in middle school that can keep a young person more alone than she or he would like to be.

The child who had playmates in elementary school can become more socially intimidated in the push and shove of middle school, when physical self-consciousness from puberty and social competition for belonging and fitting in can make creating friendships harder. As young people vie for standing, there can also be more social cruelty—teasing, rumoring, bullying, excluding, and ganging up—to assert and defend social place.

As a lonely eighth-grade informant once told me, "With all the meanness going around, middle school can be a good time not to have a lot of friends." At the same time, she had a fervent desire to have a more socially satisfying school experience. But how to accomplish this change when lack of confidence from shyness was timidly holding her back?

I suggested that, like all feelings, shyness can be very a good informant about one's unhappy state, but it can also be a very bad adviser about how to relieve it. For example, "I'm not confident mixing with people, so I'll feel better if I just keep to myself." Following fear's emotional advice only made her shyness worse.

While feelings can motivate actions, actions can also alter feelings. So the prescription for the shy middle school student lacking social confidence was to put on an act: "Pretend to be more outgoing, and you'll build confidence as you increasingly practice behaving that way." *When it comes to building confidence, there is no substitute for acting how you'd like to be.*

Competence Builds Confidence

Parents should listen for and affirm adolescent statements of competence. These express a can-do attitude and come in many forms. Sometimes making a can-do list with your adolescent who is feeling incapable can strengthen self-perception, helping the teenager appreciate all she or he can do. A few such can-do statements are:

- "I can work hard."
- "I can be of help."
- "I can keep trying."
- "I can make friends."
- "I can finish what I start."
- "I can perform publicly."
- "I can make people laugh."
- "I can plan and meet goals."
- "I can ask for and get help."
- "I can learn from mistakes."
- "I can compete to do my best."
- "I can brave doing hard things."
- "I can solve problems that arise."
- "I can speak up when I have need."
- "I can make myself do what needs doing."
- "I can keep agreements to myself and others."

One job of parents is to recognize practices that enable their adolescent to make these and other kinds of *can-do statements* that provide grounds for self-confidence. Looking at such a list, the young person might declare, "I guess I can do a lot more than I thought I could." *Competence builds confidence.*

Staying Connected Enough

The easy intimacy of their daughter's or son's childhood can spoil parents when they expect that old degree of closeness and compliance, openness and confiding, familiarity and play, and affectionate getting along to automatically continue once adolescence begins. As healthy separation begins to grow between them, some old closeness is lost. Remember: that they have lost some childhood closeness in no way prevents them from developing older grounds for closeness in the years ahead.

In addition, a parent and adolescent can still preserve a meaningful and caring connection. For example, there will usually still be a few common enjoyments worth pursuing: "We still like doing some old activities together." However, what parents used to take for granted, they may now have to work harder to encourage and maintain.

The question is an important one: How much closeness with one's adolescent is enough? Given growing distances and differences, should parents try to stay adequately connected with their more developmentally removed teenager? I believe the answer is yes. *Consider the connection challenge this way: use both conflict and contrast to connect.*

Using Conflict to Connect

It can be tempting for adults to treat increasing conflict with their teenager as a challenge to parental authority to defend against or as a contest or power struggle to win. However, to encourage ongoing intimacy with their teenager, it can be better to treat conflict—the joint willingness to contest a difference between them—as an *opportunity for constructive disagreement*. Two things are necessary for this to happen.

First, it means managing the discussion and argument so that each party can become more knowing and better known in the relationship. Second, it means jointly creating some imperfect resolution that both are willing to abide by, thereby strengthening the unity in their relationship: "It takes a lot of explaining and listening, and sometimes a bit of horse trading, but we can usually come to common terms."

Each conflict with their adolescent offers parents a choice. They can either treat a disagreement as a divider or a connector, as a barrier or a bridge, as something that is wrong in the relationship to be stopped or as something in the relationship worthwhile for investing communication into it. Not only does the safe and honest exchange of opposing views between parent and teenager enhance intimacy now, it also prepares the young person for using conflict to build intimacy in significant relationships to come.

Parents can meaningfully say to their adolescent, "Whenever we have a disagreement, and there will be more times when we shall, I want you to know that I will give you a full hearing. I will explain where I am coming from. I will answer your questions. I will try to work out a solution with you where I can, and I will always welcome coming to know you better as you grow."

Using Contrast to Connect

It can be easy for parents to treat increasing cultural contrast between the teenager's world and their own as necessarily estranging, chalking up emerging differences in enjoyments, tastes, values, and wants to a generation gap that inevitably grows them and their teenager apart. To encourage ongoing intimacy with their teenager, parents must bridge these cultural differences with interest, which means doing two things. First, it means declaring ignorance about the adolescent world today: "You're growing up in a different generation from my growing-up years." The confession of adult ignorance can confer expertise on the teenager: "I know about what my parents do not." Second, it means asking to be educated about much that is foreign to your understanding. The power of this request to be culturally educated is the positive power reversal that this request creates. Now the teenager becomes the knowledgeable teacher and the parent the ignorant student curious to know: "Could you teach me about what you know and like to do to help me to better understand?" Very different tastes in popular music can be shared in this way.

It can sometimes help if parents appreciate how many of these differences are of an experimental nature, not likely to continue into young adulthood. Although important in the moment, they are usually passingly so. So, best for parents not to panic as some unfamiliar and different expressions emerge: "But the style of dress and the hair color!" Relax: it's a trial difference, not a terminal or permanent one. However, what it represents may well be worth learning about.

Although an adolescent tends to become less intimate with parents than was the child, a lesser degree of intimacy is still worth working for to keep access open. Such close, caring, confiding company of long-trusted adults can serve that young person well, particularly during times of need: "My parents are less tuned in than they used to be, but when it matters they're always there for me. They understand me less, but they still love me as much as ever. And when I complain about not being enough, they just smile and say how I'm more than maybe I appreciate and they are glad to tell me how." ●

Chapter Seven

Rejection and Order

● ● ●

"Keeping order and following orders are harder to do!"

Separating from childhood and entering adolescence around the late elementary and early middle school years can create three growth challenges concerning order for the emerging adolescent. In each case, the young person can become more disorderly than the child she or he was.

First is more difficulty *keeping order*—for example, living in an increasingly disorganized state with a jumbled backpack or cluttered bedroom.

Second is more difficulty *following orders*—for example, becoming more prone to delay and disagreement when directed or requested by parents.

Third is more difficulty *maintaining priorities*—for example, more temptation to devalue what's important later for indulging in pleasure now.

In each case, *order is about control.*

Please keep in mind that I am not talking here about chaos, insurrection, or lack of caring, only that young people typically grow somewhat more scattered, resistant, and diverted at this changing time of life. Thus she or he can become more challenging to parents as childhood order can be rejected on any or all of these three counts. Sometimes parents take offense at what feels to them like the beginning of a more confused, resistant, and less responsible age: "She can't keep track of anything." "He questions whatever we ask." "What's most important is what's appealing now."

Best to remember that now they are living with a young person who may be pulled in more directions than in childhood, more actively and passively oppositional to live with, and at times caring more about the moment than how later matters. The parental adjustment can feel unwelcome: "Keeping her on track is harder now."

However, adolescent disorder is functional as it breaks old definitions to allow room for more individuality and independence to grow. That said, between orderly parents and a more disorderly teenager, more frequent conflicts about preserving order can arise: "Stop being so messy!" versus "Quit being so fussy!" There can be more conflicts about following an order: "Just do what you're told!" versus "Just tell me why." And there can be a more conflicts about order of importance: "Homework comes first!" versus "Winning this game matters most!"

Although order can be a touchy topic in adolescence, it is well worth parent attention because the capacities *to create order, to follow orders,* and *to order importance* are essential self-management skills that an adolescent will need to support their growing independence in the years ahead. Consider these three order issues one at a time.

Order and Organization

Part of feeling in control is being able to order what is happening, where things are, and what needs doing. With a wider range of experience opening up as the simpler, sheltered childhood world is let go and left behind, the adolescent would like to put this new complexity in comprehensible order: *I want to know what's going on.* However, more frequently not able to do so, she or he can feel disorganized, causing anxiety on that account. Thus the young person can feel at the mercy of growing changes that physically, emotionally, and socially make life more unexpected and uncomfortable. Because the adolescent world is more challenging than childhood, it's easy to feel ignorant, confused, and overwhelmed: *I can't keep up with all that's going on! I can't find it! I can't remember everything!*

As the push for more independence and personal freedom gets underway, early adolescent growth and the world of experience quickly becomes more complex. For example, middle school is more complicated than elementary school. With multiple teachers creating simultaneous instructional demands, there's more to keep track of: "The homework just piles on!" Now life becomes less simple, orderly, and in control. Meanwhile, fitting in with peers and social belonging become more competitive (*Who's going to be my friend today?*). Add to this the unpredictable and often unwelcome bodily changes (*I don't like how I look!*).

With so much to attend to, it's easy to feel more confused, scattered, and distracted, making it harder to concentrate, follow directions, and predict how things will be. Now it's easy to feel *disorganized* and confused, as more complexity creates a lot to keep up with and corral. To some degree, the early adolescent sacrifices the simplicity of childhood for the complexity of growing older.

In creating growing disorder, adolescence leads to the need for more order. Parenting teenagers is thus partly about providing a structure of responsible family rules and requirements to rattle around in, to fit into and conform to, until the young person develops an independent self-management structure of their own. Family order is instructional, offering training for developing one's personal order when eventually living independently: "My parents taught me how to play by the rules and sort and keep track of what I have to do."

The capacity to create order keeps the young person from living in confusion during a changing time, feeling anxiety when that order doesn't exist: *I don't know what's going on, where anything is, what happens next!* The young adolescent even faces the loss of established educational order when moving from elementary to middle school. *What will this be like?* wonders the young person. The short-term answer is some worry until a larger and more demanding school becomes familiar, a new social order is understood, and a new plan for personal order is created.

Learning to cope with early adolescent change requires taking more charge of ordering one's life. Assumption of this responsibility to create order breaks down into a set of demands for self-management that has many working parts, all of them involving valuable skills that parents can teach and encourage. Consider just a few of these essential ordering practices: planning, arranging, sorting, scheduling, complying, simplifying, and remembering. Creating and maintaining personal order takes a lot of work!

Personal order helps maintain a sense of control. For example, it allows a person to predict, find, recall, keep up with, and accomplish what they are in charge of and supposed to do. The more of these ordering skills a young person learns in early adolescence, the easier the adjustment to more complexity will be when coping with high school. Growing up constantly requires coping with more complexity.

In the face of more disorganization, parents can provide ongoing self-management instruction. This can mean helping the young person create procedures, follow a schedule, set prompts for remembering calendar obligations, straighten personal space, maintain track of possessions, set goals, and keep commitments: "Our job during this more complicated and distracting time is to help you pay continued attention to what needs doing."

For highly disorganized and distractible teenagers, it can be a mercy to live in a simply kept personal space: "Everything in my room is arranged where it's supposed to be and easy to find." While a messy room can feel free in the sense that no order is externally required, for some young people disorder can feel confusing and anxiety-provoking.

Disorder can also be distracting: "I can't concentrate!" "I don't know where I put it!" "I keep losing things!" "I forgot!" Parents need to help the young person learn to stay organized and show the young person how: "It's hard to keep track of all we have to do; that's why we keep things mostly picked up and keep a calendar—to know where to find things and to check for reminders. This way we feel more in charge of our life."

Parental supervision can play a supportive role here: "We will help you keep things straight in your room and schedule schoolwork. We do this so you can learn how to do this for yourself, making it easier to manage and remember what must be done." And just because an ordered bedroom today becomes disordered in the days that follow doesn't mean that parents can't insist the space be regularly picked up to keep the confusing messiness from returning.

Order and Obedience

Part of control is complying with an existing order. Parental demands limit adolescent freedom at an age when freedom matters more than ever, which is why there is commonly more teenage resistance to parental demands. There is more *passive resistance* in the form of delay: "It takes forever to get her to do anything we want." And there is more *active resistance* in the form of argument: "Everything we ask of him is up for debate."

The marching order for parents dealing with delay is not to be deterred. Patient, persistent parental pursuit can wear down passive adolescent delay: "My parents just keep after me until I finally do what they ask." Without getting upset, parents show they mean what they say by following through with what they want. This can take more time and effort with an adolescent than a child. Plus there is a larger lesson to be learned.

Human beings are social creatures who create systems for living. No individual lives independently because every person depends on a host of social orders as they conduct their lives. Thus the adolescent has to learn to follow established order to effectively function in the larger world.

- To gain acceptance, one has to conform.
- To enjoy social freedom, one has to obey laws.
- To drive a car, one has to observe traffic regulations.
- To hold a job, one has to accept employment practices.
- To get through school, one has to work with instruction.

Young people have to learn to go along to get along with orders in many human systems. The family system is where much of this getting along is taught. To do so, the teenager has to sacrifice something very dear: their personal freedom to decide what they can and cannot, must and must not do. An older adolescent who is persistently oppositional to authority, unwilling to sacrifice personal freedom to social compliance and conformity, can have a hard time making their way: "No one tells her what to do!"

Following order constitutes a very demanding set of skills for self-management that has many working parts, like cooperating, fitting in, going along, and obeying. Following order and complying with rules—whether at school or work or out in the world—is hard but essential. Rulers of the family system, parents first teach these social skills at home.

As for dealing with adolescent arguments, it's worth repeating what was mentioned earlier about parental authority. The mantra can be *"we will be firm where we have to, flexible where we can, explain the reasons for our decisions, treat your disagreement as worthy of discussion, and always listen to whatever you have to say, as long as it is said in a respectful and not hurtful way."* Cooperating with parental direction prepares the young person to work with societal authority. This said, because of growing independence, the child can find cooperation easier to accomplish than the adolescent.

While the child believed parents had the power to order and make them obey, the adolescent now knows that parents can't make them do anything or stop them without their cooperation. The adolescent thinking sounds like this: *You can tell me what, but I can decide when, and how much I give of what you want is up to me!* Timing and degree of compliance feel more like a matter of personal willingness now. Although still living on parental terms, the adolescent starts asserting more terms of her or his own.

Thus the young adolescent can become more disorderly in response to parental rules and requests, and sometimes more disobedient. More insistence may be required to get what parents want as their child becomes less readily cooperative with requests and compliant with rules: "We have to put up with more disagreement and must keep after her to get things done."

To some degree, the adolescent rebels out of childhood as parents encounter more opposition to orders. In the face of more disagreement, parents need to stand fast with important demands, follow through to completion with their requests, broker increasing differences with discussion, and maintain a family structure of rules and restraints in which the young person can responsibly grow: "Our job, during this more resistant time, is to provide you with consistent daily limits and demands on which you can securely depend."

Order and Prioritizing

Control is honoring what matters most. Keeping one's life in order can have to do with placing attention and energy on what matters most as choices made now affect choices later.

The problem is that, as the child grows, priorities can shift, particularly when entering the social maelstrom of middle school. Now social impression and social belonging and social treatment can feel more important. When so, the primary importance of working hard and performing well can take second place to personal appearance and social popularity, good looks and good friends sometimes counting for more than good effort and good grades: "Because so much else is going on, with my studies it's good enough to just get by."

So for some young people there can be an *early adolescent–middle school achievement drop* as making academic effort is discounted in comparison to the other, higher priorities. Parents can respectfully disagree:

"Middle school grades directly affect what you are encouraged to take in high school—like higher-level and advanced classes. Building your future opportunity is at stake. So, at a time when some of your interest in school performance has dropped, we will provide sufficient supervision to help you get all the work accomplished that for now you feel is less important to do. So we will keep after you to bring all assignments home, fully complete them, turn all the work in, study for tests, and check to make sure that you are fully cooperating in class. While we know you can get lost in the demanding present, we will continue to care about what matters in your future so you can too."

Thankless Parenting

Helping a young person keep adequate order, follow instructions, and keep their priorities in place are all part of the parents' thankless job. Therefore, consider three important parental responsibilities at this demanding stage of growth.

- Help your teenager stay sufficiently organized in a more distracting and complicated world: "Life is exhausting because you must continually keep track of more that is happening and that you need to do."
- Follow through on family rules and requests so that the teenager can trust that you mean what you say: "The demands we make of you are for you to support how safely and responsibly you grow."
- Maintain and insist on operating priorities now that will support important interests in the future to come: "We don't want you to make choices now that foreclose opportunities you may want later."

The Contradiction

If the issue of order in adolescence sounds contradictory, that's because it often is. The young adolescent may complain about the need for order, for being ordered, and for ordering what's most important, but without the support of these orders during a changing and complicated time, life can quickly feel out of control.

Hence the challenge for parents, who have to adjust to more adolescent disorder expressed through more disorganization, disagreement, and distraction while insisting that more capacities for imposing personal order, following social order, and preserving order of importance all be learned.

Sometimes, after a major adolescent violation of family order, parents will choose to play their trump correction card to encourage the errant teenager back into complying with family rules. In response to what their adolescent did or didn't do, parents will take away some significant freedom of action or use that requires parental provision or permission. Now this deprivation of precious freedom is used as a penalty to discourage repetition and to persuade the adolescent to behave in accordance with family rules. For example, social grounding, loss of smartphone, denial of permission, and withholding of allowance all send a powerful message of how many precious personal freedoms are still in the hands of parents. Come the young person's emancipation into independence, parents will control none of these, thus the growing incentive to govern one's own life. However, deprivation of personal freedom as a corrective can have an honorable early history.

For example, during the early childhood years, parents may correct a misbehaving or noncompliant little girl or boy by ordering a short time-out and talk-out so that the girl or boy can reflect on some misbehavior and hopefully decide not to repeat it. With the onset of the young person's adolescence, corrective deprivation can take a harder turn as parents may withhold freedom of action or use to penalize an infraction. Parents can treat deprivation of freedom as the strongest punishment they have in their arsenal of influence, to rely on when all other efforts of persuasion and correction fail to convince.

Selectively applied, deprivation may sometimes have corrective impact; however, it is easy for parents to use it excessively, and when they do, a self-defeating outcome can occur. As a go-to correction, or when they strip a teenager of all desirable freedoms, parents can set the aggrieved young person free indeed: "What do I care about your rules? Now you've got nothing else to take away!"

The parental job is to provide a stable family structure of responsible rules, limits, demands, and expectations for the adolescent to rattle around in as she or he pushes for more individuality—freedom of expression—and independence—freedom of action. At times of serious violations of the family structure, correction in the form of freedom deprivation can come into play. Parents need to use it wisely and in moderation.

In general, I believe deprivation of freedom as a corrective is best used only occasionally and kept short-term to be most effective. The longer it goes on, the easier it becomes for the adolescent to adjust to doing without. At worst, excessive deprivation can create a deep and abiding grievance and provoke angry acting out—or, as mentioned, can engender a nothing-left-to-lose attitude. Maybe a week is the outer limit for effective social deprivation to last. An exception might be evidence of drinking when driving, in which case parents may want to put off restoration of car freedom until they have sincere assurance that this unsafe infraction will not happen again.

For all of the above, I suggest using deprivation selectively, not routinely, and keeping it as a last resort only after three other corrective approaches have been tried first, as follows:

- **Discussion.** "We need to talk with you about the choice you made, why it does not work for us and needs not to happen again. But first, we want to hear your side of things, explaining what you want us to know. We will listen to all you have to say. In this case, lying to us is no more acceptable than our lying to you. So let's talk about how you can commit to honesty with us from now on."

- **Supervision.** "Since you are having a hard time consistently following this rule, we will consistently keep after you to encourage your compliance. In this case, we will be doing regular asking and checking and following though to make sure all your homework is brought home from school, is adequately done, and is faithfully turned in. If we have to, we will meet you after school and together make the rounds of teachers to help you pick it up, and we will go to school with you in the mornings together to help you turn it in. If, for any reason, you find our actions objectionable, you have only to take complete care of this school business yourself, and we will back off."

- **Reparation.** "As a consequence of doing what you should not have, you're going to have to work off the offense. Before you get to do anything you want to do, you will have a weekend task, above usual chores, to do around the home. And while you're so occupied, you can reflect about what got you into washing all these windows Saturday morning. We hope this will remind you not to take without asking and call it 'borrowing,' when our permission was neither asked for or given, as you well know." (One reason why parents shy away from using reparation is that it requires their supervision to be accomplished, and they are reluctant to do the work.)

When these strategies prove to have no corrective influence, parents then may want to put deprivation into play: "Since you continue to stay up into the early morning texting with friends, despite the lack of sleep that you are suffering, we need to take possession of your smartphone from bedtime to breakfast each day for the next week."

Even though the young adolescent can bridle against keeping order, following orders, and remaining mindful of order of importance, parental training in these three essential capacities provides a stable foundation on which the girl or boy can depend as growing complexity makes life demands more challenging to master. ●

Chapter Eight

Rejection and Intimacy

● ● ●

"I'm still close to my parents, just not as much."

The easy intimacy of their daughter's or son's childhood can spoil parents when they expect the same degree of closeness and transparency, openness and confiding, familiarity and play, and affectionate getting along to all automatically continue once adolescence begins. While the little child may have told their parents everything, the adolescent is much more selective about what is shared. In service of growing separation, with the onset of adolescence, more social and emotional distance begins to build.

Not only does adolescence grow the child out of the age of command ("My parents can control what I do") into the age of consent ("My parents can't make me or stop me without my cooperation"), it also grows the child out of the age of confiding ("I tell my parents everything") into the age of concealment ("I don't tell my parents more than is good for me"). In the process, some old intimacy with the child is lost: "We knew our child far better than we know our adolescent. She's more private than she used to be."

Why so? Increased self-consciousness from puberty, the push for more independence, growing discontent with living on parental terms, competing for attachment to peers, and managing a more complex interior world all tend to motivate this increased desire for privacy: "Now I have more to keep to myself."

Paths to Intimacy

I believe that two paths to intimacy exist in human relationships whether between dear friends, romantic or marriage partners, or parent and offspring.

- The easier path to intimacy is through combining *human similarities* to create a sense of valued commonality, establishing closeness together through sharing likeness in this companionable way: "We love how we are so alike!"
- The harder path to intimacy is through encompassing *human diversity*, tolerating and appreciating contrast, working around and with this mixture to find an enriching compatibility: "Our differences go well together!"

A parent and adolescent who say they are entirely alike and never disagree may be suppressing honest differences and sacrificing significant intimacy. For example, between an authoritarian parent with a high expectation of obedience and an anxious teenager with a high need to please, compliance can be at the expense of closeness: "With my dictatorial dad, I make myself easy to get along with but harder to truly know."

Adolescence Complicates Intimacy

Go back to the notion that when the child separates from childhood and enters adolescence, two major avenues for growth gather power. Each one can make it harder for the parent to maintain traditional intimacy with the changing young person.

As the adolescent starts *detaching from childhood and parents* for more freedom of independence, more *conflict* grows between them. And as the adolescent starts *differentiating from childhood and parents* for more individual expression, more *contrast* grows between them.

While parent/child intimacy was encouraged by both parties sharing more similarities and fewer differences, *parent/adolescent intimacy* is challenged by both parties sharing fewer similarities and encountering more differences. For this reason, parents can find the young child more endearing and the young adolescent more abrasive to live with. It's often easier for a parent to feel intimacy with an attached and similar child than with a detaching and differentiating adolescent.

So, as suggested earlier, one parenting issue question is how to turn more conflict and more contrast into more intimacy, not less. The answers are (1) conflict can be treated as an opportunity for communication and (2) contrast can be treated as an opportunity for understanding.

Conflicting Differences

It can be tempting for adults to treat increasing conflict with their teenager as an unpleasantness to tolerate, a challenge to their authority to defend against, or a contest or power struggle to win. However, to encourage ongoing intimacy with their teenager, it can be better to treat conflict (the joint agreement to contest a difference between them) as an opportunity for *constructive disagreement*.

This requires doing two things. First, it means managing the discussion and argument so that each party can become more knowing and better known in the relationship. Second, it sometimes means jointly creating some imperfect resolution that both are willing to abide by, thereby strengthening unity in their relationship: "It takes a lot of explaining and listening, and maybe some horse trading, but we can usually come to agreed-upon terms."

Each conflict with their adolescent confronts parents with a choice. They can either treat a disagreement as a divider or a connector, a barrier or a bridge, or as something wrong in the relationship to be stopped or as something at odds in the relationship worth trying to understand. The name of that bridge is "discussion." Not only does the safe and honest exchange of opposing views between parent and teenager enhance intimacy now, it also prepares the young person for using conflict to build intimacy in significant relationships to come.

Parents can say to their adolescent and mean, "Whenever we have a disagreement, and there will be more of these times, that just signifies that we have a need to talk and listen. Disagreement means we have more to discuss." At that point, the power of listening to enhance intimacy comes to the fore.

The Power of Listening

Listening is the all-purpose human relations skill. Specifically (what is expressed) and symbolically (what it can signify) listening cements relationships by allowing an exchange of nonverbal and verbal personal data that enlighten one person's understanding about another. For example, verbal communication allows one person to *speak up* and be known by another person who *shuts up* and listens. *Listening is an act of intimacy as it welcomes and deepens knowing in the relationship.* Absence of listening can be painful, as in the adolescent's complaint to a busy parent, "You never have time to listen to me!"

Just for a moment, consider a few other functions of parental listening.

- Listening is *a gift*: you are offering your attention.
- Listening shows *interest*: you are curious to know what will be said.
- Listening is *availability*: you make time to hear what someone has to say.
- Listening is *affirming*: you treat the speaker as having something worth saying.
- Listening provides *companionship*: you become a partner in discussion.
- Listening helps *processing of experience*: you encourage talking out what is happening.
- Listening creates *vulnerability*: you feel affected by what you hear.
- Listening is *supportive*: you relieve the burden of what is said.
- Listening makes *public*: you allow the personal to be confided.
- Listening is *trusting*: you each risk being better known.
- Listening is *educational*: you know more than before.

However, while listening commands attention, it does not necessarily promise agreement, nor is listening always easy. For example, listening can be hard when your mind is already made up, you don't want to hear what is being told, you must interrupt what you're busily doing, you feel upset by what you hear, you feel too tired to attend, you think you've heard this all before, you disagree with what you're told, you are impatient to act, you feel offended or accused, or you feel helpless or threatened. This reminds me of the parent who apologized to his teenager, "Sorry, my listening was broken. Please try me again."

So how might the four kinds of listening sound?

Active listening: "I really want to understand."

Reflective listening: "This is what I heard you say."

Empathetic listening: "I feel the feelings you describe."

Interpretative listening: "It sounds like you regret what happened."

Finally, not only is parental listening an all-purpose human relations skill, with an adolescent it can also be an act of love: "Even though what I said was not always what my parents wanted to know, they really heard what I had to say." Hence that most powerful adolescent compliment to parents of all: "I can talk to my folks about anything." Conflict can be a hard opportunity for listening.

Contrasting Differences

It can be easy for parents to treat increasing cultural contrast between the teenager's world and their own as necessarily estranging, chalking emerging differences in enjoyments, tastes, values, and wants up to an inevitable generation gap that grows them and their teenager apart. To encourage ongoing intimacy with their teenager, the parent must bridge these cultural differences with interest, which means doing two things.

First, bridging cultural differences with interest means declaring ignorance about the adolescent world today: "You're growing up in a very different time from my growing-up years." The confession of adult ignorance can confer expertise on the teenager: "I know about what my parents do not." Second, such connection means asking to be educated about much that is foreign to your understanding. The power of this request to be culturally educated is the positive power reversal that this request creates. Now the teenager becomes the knowledgeable teacher and the parent the ignorant student curious to know: "Could you help me appreciate the songs you love? I would really like to better understand the music that matters to you."

It can sometimes help if parents understand that many of these differences are of an experimental nature and are not likely to continue. Although important in the moment, they are usually passingly so. The best reaction for parents is not to panic as some unfamiliar and different expression emerges: "But blue highlights in his hair!" Relax: it's a trial difference, not a permanent one. However, what it represents may well be worth understanding.

Parent: "Could you help me understand why?"

Adolescent: "I just wanted to try looking this way for a while."

P: "And what have you found out?"

A: "How people judge by your appearance."

P: "And how do they judge you?"

A: "Like I'm a possible troublemaker, when I'm not!"

Although an adolescent tends to become less intimate with parents with time, a lesser degree of intimacy can still be adequate for keeping access open. Such close, caring, confiding company of long-trusted adults can serve a young person well, particularly during times of need: "My parents aren't as tuned in as they used to be, but when it matters they're still there for me."

Loss of Popularity

For some parents, the onset of adolescence (starting around ages nine to thirteen) can be dispiriting when traditional popularity with their child falls away: "My child used to like me hanging around his friends, proud to have me as his parent, happy to welcome my company with them. But now there are more times when I'm kept out, treated like a social embarrassment. Afterwards he asks me why did I have to act a certain way, why did I have to say what I said, why couldn't I leave them more alone?   I was just joining in like always, but now being part of their gathering is less okay. Just give them a friendly hello and then butt out, that's how he wants it. I've become less popular than I used to be."

As independence develops, parents are pushed more to the periphery of their adolescent's social world. From being more of an insider with the child's friends, they become more of a troublemaker as their teenager grows.

What's Going On?

Credit adolescence and the transformation it creates—developmentally changing the child, the parent in response, and the old relationship between them. Adolescence begins with loss for parents. Parents will never again have their adorable and adoring little child who doted on their company, while the adolescent must give up the perfectly wonderful parents they once idealized. Neither can ever go back to the simpler, secure, sheltered world of childhood they once shared.

When holding on becomes hanging on to what is over, it's often time to do some letting go. One common sign that parents need to let go is resenting their child for turning into an adolescent.

Rejection and Resentment

You can appreciate this doting parent's complaint about adolescent change, "From the start, my magical child and I fell in love with each other, but now it feels like he's fallen out of love with me!"

What a loss—and for some parents, it's a betrayal: "It's like I've been rejected, and I feel so hurt and angry! We were so close and now he's pushing me away. It's not right that he's doing this to me!" In this way, parental resentment at unchildlike behavior is born. *Caring about what is lost is replaced by criticism of what is missed.*

Of course, the parent is correct about rejection, but she is taking personally what is not meant to be personal. Adolescence does begin with rejection in words and actions, the child stating, "I'm no longer content to be defined and treated as just a little child anymore."

Rejection of childhood, while it can refuse some old parent behavior like public hugging and holding hands and so much social time spent together, does not express any lessening of love for the parent. Now comes a time for the parent to find different ways to demonstrate that love—for example, through providing interest and empathy, offering structure and support, and being willing to listen at a moment's notice, no matter how inconvenient.

When I suggested to one rejected/resentful parent that living with an adolescent is often different from living with a child and that some unwelcome changes might be expected, she sadly corrected me: "It feels like the old magic is gone from our relationship." Her grief had a piece of the truth because in some cases the adolescent transformation can be quite dramatic, or the parent can be largely unprepared as adolescence starts growing them apart, which is what it is meant to do.

Unwelcome Changes

None of what follows is to say that parents are destined for unhappiness when their child starts the adolescent transformation process. *They are not.* However, the young person may undergo some common changes which parents must learn to live with and expect. For example, the young person may sometimes become

- Less sensitive and more self-centered
- Less agreeable and more argumentative
- Less affectionate and more standoffish
- Less appreciative and more ungrateful
- Less compliant and more resistant
- Less cheerful and more moody
- Less conforming and more rebellious
- Less admiring and more critical
- Less companionable and more separate
- Less communicative and more secretive
- Less helpful and more uncooperative
- Less prompt and more delayed
- Less orderly and more disorganized
- Less focused and more distracted
- Less interested in family and more in friends

All these changes and many others can add up to losing a lot of beloved child characteristics for parents who, feeling injured, may turn their grief into grievance against the young person: "You used to be such a great kid. What happened to you?"

Now parental resentment criticizes and blames the adolescent for normal alterations that come with growing up, changes the adolescent is responsible for managing but is not at fault for creating. And now a young person, who to some degree is already destabilized by adolescent growth—and often more disorganized and distracted on this account—can feel deprived of parental acceptance and support at a very vulnerable time: "Well, you used to be such a great parent. What happened to you?"

It works better if parents can adjust their expectations to fit a changing developmental reality and then continue to lovingly provide a firm family structure of responsible rules and norms for their adolescent to rattle around in—as well as caring communication on which the young person can rely.

Resentment and Communication

One risk of parental resentment is reducing constructive communication. Resentment may drive frustrated parents into using inflammatory language like "lazy," "disrespectful," or "irresponsible" that can trigger an emotional response: "All you ever do is criticize me!" Resentful parents can be prone to blameful name-calling that only intensifies the interaction by using general terms that are unfit for specific problem-solving.

As mentioned in the earlier chapter about communication, it's best for these frustrated parents to avoid abstracts, generalizations, and labels about how the teenager is *being* and stick to operational terms that describe the acts, behaviors, and events that she or he is *doing*. Thus, instead of angrily focusing on "What is the matter with you?" the parent calmly addresses the specific cause for concern: "I'd like to discuss some of your choices that I disagree with so we can work something out."

What Resentment Costs

Parental resentment not only can cost intimacy with the adolescent, it can alienate the parent as well: "I'm devastated that my lovely young child has turned into such a self-centered teenager. She makes less effort with us while acting like we owe her more. I used to love her company, but now I'm more inclined to leave her alone."

Better to shun resentment. Don't take the loss personally as change that the girl or boy is doing deliberately to cause hurt, which is not the case. While early-adolescent changes certainly affect parents, they are not deliberately done *to* them. The young person is simply struggling to grow forward. *Parents should honor grief at what is lost, but don't turn it into grievance.* Mourn the loss of endearing childhood and appreciate the gift of what was given.

Treat the loss of a daughter or son's beloved childhood time together with grief—and also gratitude. A parental response that might work best is one that values the past and is excited about the future. Maybe it could sound something like this: "I just want you to know that I loved our cozy childhood time together, and am forever grateful that we had it. Now I look forward to what comes next, watching you become your own independent and individual person, and being a loving and supportive part of your growing up."

Part Two

• • •

Freedom of Association with Peers

The Middle School Years

"Friends free you up and tie you down."

Let forming a "family of friends" begin!

The world of middle school can become more taxing than the world of elementary school. Consider it this way:

"Each day there's too much to do: just staying in touch and get-ting along and fitting in and catching up and keeping up with friends who matter more, and some days most of all, who get how you are when parents often don't, doing stuff with friends you wouldn't do alone, stuff parents wouldn't understand so are better left untold, needing company of people like yourself because this is no time to be alone, not left behind and out, being popular enough, looking your age or better yet even older, looks that look okay and not put down like in the mirror in the morning when you see what's wrong you have to take to school, because your body's changing, and what choice do you have, and what will people say, and wearing the right clothes and not being embarrassed looking different, being in the know about what's happening, not out of it when you don't, or are pushed and shoved or cut by gossip to live down, picked on for how you are or how you're not, wanting a group to hang with before

school and sit with at lunch to make a daily difference in how you're treated and how you feel about yourself, and all the time teachers giving you more work, staying on your case, calling on you in class, embarrassing when you feel scary stupid, so there's more to watch out for and worry over, and more to manage, so it's harder to remember everything, doing what you're told, which is why you often don't, but somehow you get through all this and make it home to get a break when parents right away ask about your day and don't be so unfriendly, I mean what are you supposed to say when they want time to talk, and remind you about chores, and what about your homework, when you just need some time by yourself in your room, door closed to be left alone, time to check with friends, a second family who take a lot of work to keep, so much is going on, all the talk, running behind because you're always scrambling, catching up with the latest because everybody's changing, your friend today maybe not tomorrow, you never know, you know, so you better be ready because, ready or not, here it comes!"

Well, maybe that's an exaggeration, but some days not so much.

The older one grows through adolescence, the more age mates come to matter. It's not that family comes to matter less, but companionship with friends—a community of peers—comes to matter more as the need for social growth asserts itself.

Friendship can provide somewhat different benefits at different ages. In very rough sequential terms, consider how the function of friendship might change though the changes of growing up.

In *childhood*, friendship has to do with having *playmates*, people around your age with whom to have fun together. There are common pleasures to be shared. There is friendship in *playful company.*

In *adolescence*, friendship has to do with joining *peers*, people around your age with whom you can socially connect. There is a common group identity to gain and to claim. There is friendship in *social membership.*

In *young adulthood*, friendship has to do with finding a social *partner* to create an intimate union. There is a primary person with whom to share life's journey. There is friendship in *committed love.*

Of course, these types of friendship are not simply sequential; they are cumulative in the sense that an important relationship, like a middle school best friendship, might comprise parts of all three—someone who is playmate, peer, and partner at the same time: "We enjoy doing stuff together, we think the same, and we like each other best." This is why when a breakup occurs, as it often does as individual change unfolds, there is so much to lose for the person left behind. So much of the attachment that can be gained can also be lost when relationships are realigned as individual change occurs: "I just outgrew that friendship and needed to move on."

That said, the companionship of friends is usually essential to adolescent growth because this community provides a social location from which further detachment and differentiation from childhood and parents can develop: *"I was raised by my parents, but I grew up with my friends."* This is why parents can feel socially demoted as peers become increasingly influential. This is also why welcoming their adolescent's friends when they drop by can create a measure of knowing that can lessen parental ignorance: "Getting to know his friends helps us better know our teenager."

Chapter Nine

Association and Separation

• • •

"I need more space from my parents."

As desire for contact time with peers becomes more socially important for the adolescent, contact time with parents can become less eagerly sought. Why? Is some kind of competition going on? In a way, yes.

Growing social independence requires letting go some of the security of old attachments, which includes more growing apart from parents. This is hard to do without developing a competing social attachment to friends that helps offset the primary loss from letting go old ties to home and childhood.

Thus, to some degree, the adolescent passage requires letting go of parents and nurturing the growing desire for time with peers, The onset of adolescence can begin to separate the relationship between parent and child in five powerful ways, some previously mentioned, each allowing more differences and distance to begin to grow between them.

Repositioning with Parents

Consider five *shifts in relationship to parents* that usually occur to some noticeable degree:

- Adolescence grows the child out of the age of command ("My parents can control what I do") into the age of consent ("My parents can't make me or stop me without my cooperation"). So there can be more disagreement.

- Adolescence grows the child out of the age of confiding ("I tell my parents everything") into the age of concealment ("I don't tell my parents more than is good for me"). So there can be less disclosure.

- Adolescence grows the child out of the age of complimenting ("My parents are mostly wonderful") into the age of criticizing ("My parents often aren't always that great"). So there can be more complaints.

- Adolescence grows the child out of the age of companionship with parents ("My folks are the most fun") into the age of comradeship with peers ("My friends fit best for me"). So there can be less time together.

- Adolescence grows the child out of the age of commonality with parents ("We mostly agree on what matters") into the age of contrast to parents ("A lot of what we value is not the same"). So there can be more cultural differences that set them apart.

On all five counts, to some degree, more social distance between parents and their adolescent will occur: "She still likes being with us but wants more time alone and apart." Adolescence causes separation, plain and simple: "Increasingly, we live our life our way, he lives his life his way, and the two are less the same." There is a growing divide.

As adolescence unfolds, parents can notice more social distance from their adolescent in a couple of telling ways: the young person wants more privacy from them, and the young person seeks to spend more time in her or his bedroom apart from family.

The Privacy Conflict

As the young person pushes for more independence and individuality, a growing tension can arise when, for freedom's sake, the adolescent has a need to be less well known by parents, who, for their own sake, have a greater need to know what is happening in their teenager's more worldly and riskier life. Adolescent privacy can become a more contested area of their relationship:

"My life is my business!"

"But you still need to tell us what's going on!"

What is the best way for parents to get the information they want? Just ask, right? No, that is often wrong. While the child may have welcomed parental questions as statements of interest, the adolescent can see the same queries in very intrusive and unwelcome terms— *as invasive of privacy and emblematic of authority.* Many teenagers become expert at the minimal and vague response:

"Even when we ask nicely, we get told precious little!"

"I said things were okay. What else is there to tell?"

So, what is a better way to satisfy the parental need to know?

Parents might consider asking fewer questions to meet their information needs and show respect for the teenager's right to control their own data. *Employ courtesy by making a request instead:* "If you could tell me more, I could be more sensitive to the situation." "I would love to better understand what that experience was like." "Knowing a little more about what happened would really ease my mind."

Parents who feel they have a right to know might object, "That's like treating our teenager talking to us like he's doing us a favor!" I agreed. "He's deciding to let you in on his private life, and he doesn't have to." Then I suggest that when any information is forthcoming, they express appreciation for being told: "Thank you for explaining and letting us know."

Consider the son who was proud to have parents watch his elementary school sports, but not anymore. Now he's making an "invisible spectator" request: "If you have to watch my game, please sit off to the side where I can't see you, don't make a lot of noise cheering, and afterwards don't come down and congratulate me. Just go to the car. I'll meet you there." At an acutely self-conscious middle school age, public association with parents can feel socially embarrassing with peers.

Privacy from Parents

Sometimes an adolescent can believe that the more privacy is kept, the freer she or he becomes. This is the notion that "parents are best kept in the dark." Actually, the opposite is true. Parents can explain, "When you keep us ignorant about what's going on, treating privacy like secrecy, our not knowing causes us to become harder for you to live with. Lack of information causes our imagination to worry about a lot of worst-case possibilities. For example, in ignorance, we may suppose you are in some kind of trouble or danger. Reaching this scary conclusion, we may feel inclined to reduce your freedom to keep you safe. Now we may become more distrustful and restrictive to live with—the opposite of what you want. The less we're told, the more protective we may become. So, it really is in your best interests to keep us adequately and accurately informed. Of course, how much you decide to tell us is entirely up to you."

Limits of Privacy

I believe parents also need to make this kind of statement about the *limits of privacy*:

"While we want to respect your privacy, it is most important that you do *not* stay private from us in certain cases.

"Please tell us when you are emotionally suffering.

"Please tell us when you feel threatened or in danger.

"Please tell us when you feel overwhelmed by so much going on.

"Please tell us when you don't know what to do about a problem.

"Please tell us when you feel isolated, helpless, and alone.

"Please tell us when you feel in trouble and don't know how to get out.

"Please tell us when you feel you can't face up to what you did.

"Please tell us when you can't stop hurting yourself.

"Please tell us if you feel you can't take any more pressure.

"We are your parents and we love you and we want to be there for you, but we can't if you don't allow us in or you keep us out. Please don't let your desire for privacy get in the way of getting our help when you have need. In these cases, we promise to listen without upset or criticism, just with loyal care, to provide the support and company you need."

Bedroom Privacy

Just as spoken privacy ("I don't want to talk about that") can protect how much is shared, physical privacy can create freedom from observation ("I keep others out by closing my door"). The major symbol of privacy for adolescents at home is their bedroom, where they can separate from family, be unbothered and unseen.

The adolescent bedroom functions in many ways for freedom: as a storage place for one's belongings, as a sanctuary from social contact, as an exhibition space of what personally matters, as an entertainment place for company, as an activity place for schoolwork and online play, and as a communication center for connecting virtually with friends. By all measures, it is usually the most important room in the home for the adolescent: "My room is where I'm free to be by myself."

Parents need to respect the adolescent bedroom because it is a sensitive matter—protective, reflective, and supportive of the growing person. Yet parents wonder: how much privacy of personal space should they allow? In general, privacy protects several freedoms: *freedom from being known, freedom for personal expression,* and *freedom of action.* In each case, parents need to let the teenager know what expectations are in place.

Basically the young person's bedroom becomes increasingly emblematic of youthful determination to live more on her or his own terms within the family. It becomes a private personal sanctuary into which to retreat from the complexities and worries of daily life. It becomes a place from which increasingly important relationships with peers can be securely conducted. To a degree, the teenage bedroom asserts social separation in the home.

- The message of the adolescent bedroom can be more separatist and territorial, "It's my space!"
- Parental presence in the adolescent bedroom can now be less welcome than before, as if it were now posted, "No adults allowed!"
- The bedroom door that mostly was publicly open in childhood

can become the door that is more often closed, "I'm busy!"

- The child who liked being at home with family can now prefer time at home alone, "Don't bother me!"
- The child who treated the bedroom as a storage place for playthings can now become a gallery to display cultural preferences, "It shows how and who I am!"
- The child who accepted parental inspection can now act like she or he owns the space, "You have no right!"

I think it's best to clarify parental expectations about adolescent room use sooner than later. The longer parents wait to set these expectations, the harder doing so may become. By middle school is the time to have "the talk." I don't mean about sex or drugs but about expectations for managing the growing power of the bedroom in your adolescent's personal life and in your family life.

One way to do so is to clarify to what degree you subscribe to extreme room rights that an adolescent might claim in the name of growing social independence, some of which are as follows:

- "The state of order I choose to keep my room in is up to me."
- "Keeping my door closed to keep others out is up to me."
- "What I keep in my room is up to me."
- "What I do online in my room is up to me."
- "How I decorate my room is up to me."
- "How loud I play music in my room is up to me."
- "Who is allowed into my room is up to me."
- "Food and dishes I leave in my room are up to me."
- "When I come out of my room is up to me."
- "Who and how I entertain in my room is up to me."

If you have a problem with any such self-assumed "rights," then declare up front what you believe instead are reasonable and healthy family expectations.

At an adolescent extreme would be the anarchic bedroom: "My room is my space to keep any way I want, and the door is always closed because it's off-limits, so keep out!" Now the bedroom is used to discourage parental supervision and family association. Most parents would refuse to live with a teenage bedroom on these prohibitive terms.

Instead, parents might declare terms of their own: "What you do in your room, what you have in your room, who you entertain in your room, how you keep your room, admission to your room—these are all partly up to us because your room is in our home, and you are still a daily part of our family, and while we will knock on a closed door, we will not be denied entry. You may expect us to freely come and go, and to some degree supervise your bedroom like we routinely do the rest of your life so long as you live with us."

Just remember that in making such a declaration you will be bumping up against the two fundamental drives that propel adolescent growth: detachment from childhood and family for more freedom of action and differentiation from childhood and family to develop a uniquely fitting identity.

The adolescent bedroom is a power place in both regards. Parents vary in how much of this power will be allowed—from the disregarding parents who prefer to look the other way to those who daily check on bedroom maintenance.

One way for parents to think about the appearance of the adolescent's bedroom is as a reflection of their teenager—a changing gallery of what matters at an age of passionate identifications and attachments that teens can communicate in a variety of extremely telling ways. In posters on the walls, for example, parents can see images and icons that have a lot to say about the person posting them, just like favorite music for current teens is worth a listen: "What he likes is what he's like, at least for the moment, so it's worth noticing and knowing about."

Sometimes extreme expressions communicated can put parents off, but adolescent redefinition is not drawn to moderation or compromise the way adults often are. All-or-nothing statements have more dramatically redefining power than settling for a middle ground, as adults have grown accustomed to do. It's generally best for parents to keep in mind that these expressions, interests, and identifications are more of a trial than a permanent nature. They serve the cause of growing up more than reflecting how the young person will actually turn out once reaching adulthood. So it is usually better to take an interest rather than to act alarmed.

Bedroom Intervention

When might parents want to exercise some influence over the extreme disorder in which a teenager's room appears? Consider three possibilities.

If you have a young person who suffers from disorganization and distractibility, adding confusion to an already more confusing age, parents can regularly help the young person keep her or his personal space in a simple and orderly state: "It's one part of my life where I can count on knowing where everything is and I feel in control."

If you have a young person whose life may be becoming chaotic but you don't know why, an extremely messy room can be exploited to keep parents out. The disorder may be intended to mask something secret that, if discovered, would reveal what is endangering or otherwise compromising. Parents should feel entitled to inspect the space when concerns arise: "We went searching among the debris and this is what we found."

If you have an extremely rebellious young person for whom a chaotic room is meant to symbolize the determination to live at home on more anarchic terms, it can be wise to go for a two-way accommodation: "Here's the deal: on the weekend we'll keep after you to put your room into sufficient order to suit our household needs; then we'll leave you mostly alone about the order or disorder you like to maintain for the next five days."

Of course, keeping after an adolescent about the state of her bedroom has both specific and symbolic power: "Keeping after my personal space just shows how my parents still mean to run my life." And keep after it they may when insisting on sufficient family membership requirements like participation in family gatherings, following basic family rules, contributing to household chores, and like helping family others when there is need.

For many teenagers, an honest sign of changing times affixed to the outside of their door might read, "ROOM TO GROW: Do not disturb." In response, parents can promise to let go and to hold on—to respect it on one hand and to inspect it on the other.

Increasing privacy and the growing power of the bedroom are only two of many adolescent changes that flower during the middle school years that parents typically encounter as stronger adolescent needs for separation grow. Now what parents have to manage from growing separation is often *more frustration* with their child than they have experienced.

Parental Frustration

Consider this very human declaration as more teenage independence and individuality grows:

"I tend to be fairly patient as a parent, but I find myself feeling so frustrated and angry at teenage behavior. I even wake up in the morning just seething—like just trying to control the situation, I guess. I just wish I could get it through their head to listen to me. I think one of the biggest frustrations with the teen years, though, is that they also argue rationally! So I can't win as easily.

"Like I might tell my teen, 'You have to wear clean clothes because people will judge you or you could get sick, etc.' And the teen will argue, 'But people don't care about that, and I don't want people to judge me by my appearance.' Well fine, but still it makes life harder.

"Or, 'You have to go to sleep at X time' and it's, 'But I can't force myself to go to sleep, can I?' It's like, 'No, but you have to try.' 'But why try to do something that's impossible? Are you saying you can just will yourself to sleep?' UGH!

"Even though I've never thought of myself as an angry person, I've been so frustrated lately. It's become very disruptive to my own well-being first, and also to my teen. So dealing with my own frustration is really important to everyone."

It's easy for parental frustration with growing adolescent separation to create a feeling of anger at being denied that turns into resentment at the teen for upsetting the parent. Now everyone suffers emotionally.

The Danger of Frustration

The danger of frustration for parents facing an oppositional teenager is that it can be inflammatory, leading to emotional escalation.

With more intensity, feelings are increasingly allowed to control "thinking." In this aroused state, parents become less able to listen and more at risk of extreme words and actions, while the teenager, because conflict creates resemblance, can feel encouraged by example to ramp up resistance in response. Now each runs the risk of losing it to win the encounter, a bad outcome all the way around.

Should parents find themselves in a state of rising frustration with their teenager, the best advice is *separate, don't escalate*. While the teenager may only be driven to keep going, the parent needs to be motivated to restore calm. The parent can declare a short time-out, creating a break for both to recover their better judgment and then reengage in a specified while when cooler heads can prevail.

Keeping One's Cool

As a child grows into adolescence, emotional demands on parents can often increase. Why?

While it takes a lot of emotional energy to help a child securely attach to his or her parents, it can take even more emotional energy to stay well connected to a teenager once the ten- to twelve-year-long adolescent transformation ending in young adulthood is underway.

Consider some teenage separation changes with which parents must contend and some emotional demands on parents while these changes are unfolding:

- As the young person pushes for more independence, parents can feel less in control and more insecure.
- As the young person expresses more individuality, parents can feel less tolerant and more critical.
- As the young person pulls away for more privacy and separation, parents can feel more distant.
- As the young person experiments more with the forbidden

and unknown, parents can feel more anxious.

- As the young person acts more resistant to parental authority, parents can feel more challenged.

Because on all counts parents are now living in a more emotionally intensified state with their adolescent, self-management of their intensity is extremely important. It affects how they communicate and act. This not only impacts the young person directly, it can often encourage an adolescent to imitate the example parents set. Parents who can keep their *emotional sobriety* with their more provocative and unpredictable adolescent teach their teenager to operate the same. What is emotional sobriety, and why does it matter?

Emotional Sobriety

By "emotional sobriety," I refer to *the parental capacity, when pressed or challenged in the relationship with their adolescent, to remain realistically focused and not allow emotional upset to rule.* Parents remain

- **Calm** (they do not raise their voice).
- **Caring** (they do not become hostile).
- **Focused** (they do not stray from the specific issue at hand).
- **Reasoned** (they do not sacrifice judgment to feeling's rule).
- **Relaxed** (they take a time-out and do not allow upset to build).

As mentioned earlier but worth repeating here, lose emotional sobriety in the moment, and spoken language can change for the worse in three common ways.

1. Choice of words can change from *operational* ("This is what you did") to *evaluative* ("This shows how you are").
2. Choice of words can change from moderate ("This is what you sometimes do") to *extreme* ("This is what you always do").

3. Choice of words can change from acceptance ("This is our problem") to *attack* ("This is your fault!").

With parents and an adolescent who are caught in a hard place with each other and are emotionally slugging it out in counseling, one role for the counselor is to help them restore more constructive communication with each other. "Let your feelings dictate your language, and your language will only intensify your own and each other's emotions."

One of the best definitions of emotional sobriety I ever heard is "grace under pressure," President John F. Kennedy's statement about the challenge of leadership in a time of crisis. I believe the same definition applies to parental leadership with their changing adolescent. It can take a huge amount of self-discipline for parents not to lose patience with an impulsive or intense adolescent so that cooler thinking and better judgment, and not reactive feelings, can rule.

Maintaining emotional sobriety takes practice. Consider a grandmother caretaking two teenage grandchildren who explained how she never used punishment as a corrective when either young person went astray. "Coffee talks" were her solution. When a misdeed or a mistake occurred, she slowed family functioning down by taking her time and their time by announcing it was time for her to get a cup of coffee. Then they would sit down for however long it took to talk out what happened, consider why, figure out how to deal with the consequences, and make sure it didn't happen again: "From learning to do this with their mom, I learned to keep it with my grandkids."

In parenting adolescents, maintaining emotional sobriety can take practice, but it's definitely worth the effort. Now it's time to return to an earlier topic: *expectations.*

Frustration = Violated Expectations

What exactly is frustrated when frustration occurs?

The explanation often is what has been touched upon earlier: *expectations*. For instance, what you thought would be easy to do or immediately forthcoming proves hard to do or is not occurring. Frustration is the emotion linked to "not getting my way," a very human, felt response to delay, denial, or blockage of the three kinds of expectations: ambitions, predictions, and conditions.

- *Ambitions*—when what a parent *wants* to happen doesn't happen: "I wanted her to remember my birthday, and she forgot it." Frustration can feel like a let down. Now the parent can feel inclined to blame the adolescent for disappointing them.
- *Predictions*—when what a parent anticipates *will* happen doesn't happen: "I assumed he'd keep his word and he didn't." Frustration can feel like a surprise. Now the parent can feel inclined to blame the adolescent for causing them anxiety.
- *Conditions*—when what a parent believes *should* happen doesn't happen: "She knows the rules and still did wrong." Frustration can feel like betrayal. Now the parent can feel inclined to blame the adolescent for making them angry.

While it's tempting to blame emotional upset from violated parental expectations on the adolescent, it's important for parents to remember that they are responsible for expectations they set.

Expectations Are Functional

When an ambition, prediction, or condition is unmet, frustration can result. So does that mean parents shouldn't have expectations? No. Expectations are functional. They are essential mental sets that people depend on to make their way through time and change with some sense of what they would like and what is likely to occur. Expectations are a conceptual bridge to the future to help make the present more manageable. They are one way of thinking ahead.

However, expectations are mental sets with powerful emotional consequences, particularly when violated, so parents need to choose them carefully. *Part of the art of parenting is changing expectations to fit the changing reality of the growing child.* Parents who are locked into a childhood set of expectations can find older adolescent behavior very frustrating to live with; a lot of normal changes can feel wrong: "She tells us less about herself now." "He no longer likes to be hugged." "She prefers time with friends over family." "He just holes up in his room." "She spends endless time getting ready to go out." "He's more critical of the ways we are." "She takes forever to do what we ask." "He'll argue about the time of day."

Increasing change in the adolescent constantly violates old parental expectations, with adult frustration often the result. Now a relevant question becomes "Is my teenager doing something wrong, or are my expectations of teenage behavior out of line?"

While a natural parental response to adolescent violation is "Why did you do that?" a better one can be "What was I expecting?" After all, expectations are not genetically fixed; they are consciously chosen. Best for parents to take responsibility for their own frustration and ask themselves, *Was my expectation realistic?* and *Do I want to continue to hold this expectation, or do I want to change it?*

The problem with blaming parental frustration on the teenager is that parents give that young person control over their emotions, can feel victimized, and are more at risk of saying hurtful words in response. While it's hard to remember, please do so: *no one and nothing can frustrate you without your permission.*

Moderating Parental Frustration

To moderate parental frustration with your adolescent, manage your expectations mindfully. Here are some suggestions:

- Keep communicating specific expectations for healthy conduct.
- Keep asking for needed information so that you can know what to expect.
- Treat your expectations as approximations, not absolutes.
- Adjust your expectations to fit growing adolescent changes.
- Don't take violations of expectations as personal affronts.
- Don't blame your feelings of frustration on the adolescent.
- Take emotional responsibility when violated expectations occur.
- Reset healthy expectations after a violation has been addressed.

End with this piece of adolescent advice to his dad: "Well, if you just didn't expect me to be perfect, you wouldn't get upset with me all the time!"

Because adolescent development ordains increasing separation so that more freedom of independence can grow, some frustration over control naturally occurs. Parents can feel a loss of traditional influence, while the adolescent can feel denied sufficient freedom. Thus, to some degree the age-old conflict unfolds: between adult restraint ("You'll do what you're told!") and youthful resistance ("I'll do what I decide!"). Usually by middle school, adolescent separation has already created frustration for parents and the adolescent.

Since both parent and adolescent have more cause for mutual frustration from separation by this age, parents need to model how to manage normal frustration. If they lose their temper to frustration, the teenager is likely to learn this example when managing frustration on her or his side. However, if adults treat frustration as a time to talk out and work out whatever friction over growing freedom from separation is going on, that encourages the young person to do the same.

Frustration and Violence

When parental frustration feels overwhelming, acts of violence can occur. By "violence" I mean any parental act of verbal or physical aggression committed with the hostile intent of inflicting hurt on the child. In words and actions, violence communicates a lot. Let's differentiate between verbal and physical violence by starting with verbal violence first.

The old adage "sticks and stones can break my bones but words can never hurt me" is untrue. In counseling folks, I've heard endless examples of the hurt that harsh words can do. Name-calling, threats, insults, yelling, ridicule, embarrassment, humiliation, criticism, and belittling can all be acts of violence that inflict psychological harm: "I know I'm worthless because my parents often told me so."

Most of the damage in caring relationships is inflicted through speech. Examples of spoken violence to their teenager include "You should be ashamed of yourself!" "You're so lazy!" "You can't do anything right!" "What a dumb thing to do!" "You'll never learn!" "You're nothing but a failure!" "What a loser!" Such verbal violence from people as powerful as parents can injure an adolescent's sense of self and damage self-esteem: "I never lived up to my parents' expectations, and I never will."

Physical violence is more bluntly expressed. It takes advantage of the parent's larger size and family standing to use forcefulness to intimidate or dominate the child. It can be in the form of grabbing, squeezing, shaking, slapping, shoving, hitting, belting, or beating.

Sometimes justified as punishment or indulged in to feel powerful or as an outlet for angry feelings, physical violence from parents can inflict specific and symbolic harm: "That showed her how I mean what I say!"

Thus for the teen, specifically it can cause emotional and physical pain: "Acting angry they could really hurt me." Symbolically it can show how parental might is right: "And don't you forget it!"

The Costs of Violence

Parental violence can be costly in many ways.

For the child victim, parental violence can feel unsafe, unloving, frightening, and destructive. It can inflict injury, create danger, foster distrust, cause suffering, alienate affections, and be long remembered. Add up all these and its other effects, and the sum can become a badly injured relationship.

Violence in either form abuses parental power. Parenting is always partly about the management of superior power with children, and I believe resorting to violence is an abuse of that authority. At the very least, trust is lessened in the safety that parents should provide.

As for parents, blaming the victim is not the answer: "You drove me to it!" or "You made me that angry!" Such excuses misplace adult responsibility. In grievance, desperation, or frustration, parents abandoned working out a problem *with* the child for acting out *against* the child.

Parents who believe in corrective violence, like spanking for misdeeds (which I personally disagree with), need to be sure that in doing so they do not cross the line where child safety is lost and lasting injury is given. As a precaution, *never spank in anger* because now you are "thinking" with your feelings, not using your judgment, and are more at risk of making an excessive response. Frustration can turn into anger and become dangerous, seen as a precursor or justifier of violence: "When my parent gets angry, I know I better watch out!"

Later Consequences

Finally, most of what parents have to give their child is, through instruction, example, and interaction, who and how they are. In response to parental violence, the child victim can learn a formative lesson for later caring relationships. When such patterning occurs, the grown child victim may become violent in an adult relationship, enter a relationship with a violent partner, or become violent with children, repeating responses learned long ago.

For example, identifying with violence the adult might explain, "I hit my partner like my parent hit me." Adjusting to violence, the adult might explain, "I appease my violent partner like I did my violent parent." With adolescents, a parent may say, "I treat my kids no differently than my parents did me."

People often don't just get what they want in grown relationships; they can also get what is (and feels) familiar: "I end up yelling at my kids like my parents did with me!" This is why the regretful parent sought counseling—to learn a more constructive response to adolescent opposition.

For all these reasons, I am opposed to parental violence. My advice is that should you ever find yourself inclined to be violent with your child, stop your action immediately and take a break to figure out—maybe get help to find—a nonviolent other way. And if acts of parental violence have occurred, get some reconciliation counseling for you and your child together to work through the damages done and commit to never doing it again. ●

Chapter Ten

Association and Membership

• • •

"Suppose I have no friends?"

Most young people seem to know that adolescence is no time to go it alone. Such social isolation can breed loneliness and ignorance: "I don't have friends to hang with." "No one tells me anything!" Adequate company is important for adolescents to keep. An adolescent peer group is the collection of friends with whom a young person regularly hangs out.

While the pressure of peer group membership (to agree, conform, fit in, follow, or keep up with, for example) can sometimes endanger an adolescent or lead him or her astray, it can also be an essential contributor to a young person's growth, with both educational and developmental value.

Peer group membership can empower the teenager in multiple ways. It provides social belonging: "I'm part of a crowd." It gives social support: "I can depend on others." It fosters freedom: "I do what I wouldn't alone." It increases social skills: "I practice give-and-take." It confers identity: "I am who I run with." It asserts independence: "I have a separate social life from family."

Peer group membership, however, can also complicate parenting an adolescent.

Two Social Families

Most teenagers grow up in two families, not one—the parental family and the friend family. The peer group, the latter, gathers social power as the young person grows. Thus one important task of parents come adolescence is to create a positive connection with their teenager's social family, which sometimes can mean including a teenager's friend in a family occasion or just creating a comfortable place where her or his friends can hang out. It often helps to have snack food available "to feed the troops," as one father put it when an assortment of familiar and unfamiliar faces dropped by after school.

It's not that as a parent you're trying to become friends with your teenager's friends and be one of the group; you are not. But you can be an interested, accepting, and welcoming adult whose home place feels like a safe and relaxing place to gather. And you can even assert some rules: "It's good to see you. By the way, we are a cigarette-free home and so would appreciate your not smoking here. Food's in the other room. Eat up!" Enjoying a teenager's friends can also powerfully signify to their adolescent, "Liking my friends also shows how they like me."

When Parents Get Scared

Because they are social outsiders to their teenager's peer group, parents can sometimes feel threatened by its competitive influence:

"Suppose the crowd she runs with puts her at risk or gets her in trouble?" Now their biological family feels less influential than their teenager's social family: "One of her close friends, one of her group, just had a drinking-and-driving crash. We don't want that to happen to her!"

But if parents criticize or attack the friend or group, they can alienate their daughter whose social loyalty she may feel obliged to defend: "You've never liked who I hang out with! My friends are me!" So parents explain, "We don't dislike your friend. We're sorry for her. We're not attacking her. We're just wishing that you can learn from her unhappy experience so you can avoid it yourself."

Peer Groups Are Cultural

Often of the same sex, peer groups are culturally laden by shared similarities among members, so parents can tell something about their teenager's current values, focus, and beliefs by the crowd around her or him. Peer groups can provide a source of companionship and a collective identity: "We are me!" At least for the moment, the group provides some common interest or belonging that personally matters. Membership secures the growing young person, who feels supported by the like company she or he keeps.

If parents are concerned that this affiliation will be a lasting one, they usually need not worry. For example, the alternative rad or goth affiliation now so passionately embraced is most likely to pass as youthful members grow older and socially disperse. These are typically trial, not permanent, definitions, cast off when no longer of personal use.

Social Demotion

As friends grow more important in adolescence and as peer group membership increasingly preoccupies teenage attention, parents can feel socially demoted: "Friends come first for him and we come last." "When she's at home, she's not at home, but texting or networking with friends." However, this second family of friends has transitional value. It enables social separation from parents that empowers independent growth, which is what adolescence is about. Now the young person is creating and managing her or his own fitting social world.

Just because time with parents is less of a priority doesn't mean that parents are not still fundamentally important for their abiding love, interest, and support. It's just that friends are increasingly a better social fit than parents, peers are into current interests that parents are not, and the demands and pleasures of creating a separate social life increasingly call more strongly than family life. Now parents gradually begin that final task of parenting an adolescent: to keep emotionally holding on with steadfast love, while starting to back off for the final social letting go.

Peer Groups Complicate Parenting

As discussed, sometimes parents worry or even take offense when, compared to childhood, their teenager is more preoccupied with peers and less interested in being with them. However, becoming socially connected with friends is an important stepping-stone to more social independence. A band of buddies can anchor social growth during a changing time by providing a welcome sense of belonging, stability, identity, and support, whether one is in a peer group or a social clique.

The difference between the two designations can be an experiential one. A rough distinction might be this. While a *peer group* can feel more inclusive, tolerant, and relaxing ("I just like to hang out with them"), a *clique* can feel more exclusive, conforming, and demanding ("I have to keep up with them to belong"). Both provide socially anchoring experiences, with a peer group feeling freer than a clique.

Differing Worlds

While parents can love their adolescent, and it's important they do, these adults don't usually understand more of what matters to their teenager as adolescence unfolds. A cultural generation gap helps widen the growing social separation between the more traditional parent and the more contemporary teenager. To keep this growing chasm from leading to estrangement, parents can do a couple of things.

First, as mentioned earlier, parents can declare honest ignorance in what interests their teenager, who now has a lot to teach them about growing differences—if they express a desire to be taught: "Can you help me appreciate the music you love listening to now?" Second, parents can welcome their teenager's friends into the home so that these companions are not distrusted as threatening strangers, but are positively familiar and can help you better understand your teenager's world: "It turns out that her new friend, who some days dresses like an urban outlaw, is really a sweet person underneath." This welcoming can also create a plus side for your teenager because having "cool" parents can be a compliment to your daughter or son: "We like hanging out at your place."

Groups and Growth

Membership in peer groups plays a functional role in furthering the two major goals of adolescent development.

First, peer group membership provides relationships where one can *detach* from childhood and family and become more *independent*. Affiliation with a peer group increases social separation from childhood and parents: "I want to spend more time with friends and less with my family."

Second, peer groups provide a place where one can *differenti-ate* from childhood and family and become more of an *individual*. Adopting popular tastes and identifying with popular icons increases the contrast with childhood and parents: "What I like is less similar to what my parents do."

In both cases, hanging with age mates allows redefinition of one-self in older terms. In the larger picture, the social growth progression seems to be as follows:

- In childhood, you draw much definition from similarity to parents.
- In adolescence, you draw more definition from similarity to peers.
- In young adulthood, you design definition more on your own terms.

In this progression, peer group membership plays an essential preparatory role. In adolescence you are no longer a child and not yet an adult, letting go of the former and preparing for the latter. Peer groups provide much education, company, and support as one engages with the demands of this transitional change.

Parents often fear the trouble a peer group can get their child into, risking with others what one wouldn't dare alone. This can be true. However, in many cases of adolescent risk-taking, friends watch over each other and can be protective: "I could have been hurt if it wasn't for my friends." "They were the ones who brought me safely home." *Peers can look after each other.*

There is also the benefit of vicarious learning from hearing about other people's experiences: "I know what that's like from what my friends said." "I was told enough about it not to want to try it." In peer groups a lot of experience is shared not just by doing together but also by just talking together. Young people learn from hearing about each other's lives. What to do, how to do, what to watch out for, what not to do are all discussed. There are lots of topics a young person likes to talk about with peers that she or he would be far less inclined to discuss with parents. *Peers can educate each other.*

Of course, there is the problem of peer misinformation: what a young person is told by a trusted youth informant isn't the case. Thus parents do need to keep an ear out for misguiding hearsay: "You can't be charged for that if you're under eighteen." "A drug can't hurt you if you take it in very small amounts." "You can't get pregnant if you do it the first week after your period." This is why parents need to speak to basic safety issues around common issues like legal standing, substance use, and sexual behavior.

Peer Group Pressure

Peer groups are not without influence, even though less commandingly so than cliques. When groupthink in the moment takes over, with most everyone excited about some appealing possibility, it can feel hard to be the only one to resist immediately going along. Out goes the cry, "It's boring having nothing to do, so let's just go and try this!" What now?

First, teens can play for delay. Ask some questions to create discussion. If one person doesn't want to do it, it's likely some others also feel unsure or the same. Discussion can create doubt. An adolescent can also take a bathroom break to create time to think, and while away the group impulse to act may have passed. Sometimes parents can offer absentee help for these pressing moments: "If you ever get in a social situation where you don't want to do what others are suggesting, but it's really hard to refuse, you can always lie and use us an excuse: 'If I went along with this and my parents found out, they would ground me forever! So for me, it's not worth doing.'"

On balance, I believe it's freer to grow up in a peer group of friends than without one.

Social Cliques

A social clique is a group defined around some shared values, characteristics, or purpose that allows members to set themselves apart from others. Most cliques are closed groups because they are *exclusively* defined: "We are not they, and they are not us." Membership is limited, decided by those who already belong.

Cliques come in many forms. For example, the cliques can be based on lifestyle, culture, popularity, wealth, gangs, athletics, or gaming, or whether someone is an alternative, a stoner, a skateboarder, or whatever. Socially, the clique has a lot to offer. For example, cliques can provide

- **Commonality**—one feels social similarity
- **Security**—one feels social protection
- **Identity**—one has social definition
- **Belonging**—one has a social home
- **Loyalty**—one feels social allegiance
- **Standing**—one feels social importance

From what I've seen of the adolescent passage, social cliques are most powerful in middle school. Why so? During this vulnerable age, there is a great growing developmental insecurity, for several reasons:

- Increased separation from childhood and parents, so one feels more lonely and disconnected

- Uncertain and often unwelcome physical changes of puberty, so one often feels more inadequate and uncomfortable

- More social meanness (teasing, rumoring, exclusion, bullying, ganging up) as young people jockey for their social place, so one feels more exposed and vulnerable

At this changing stage of life, forming a second family of friends becomes increasingly important to create and maintain acceptance, confidence, and stability: "I need a separate social life from home."

Cliques can feel cool when you belong and cruel when you don't. That's one of the problems with cliques. They can cut both ways. Acceptance is based on similarity to what is prized that members should personify and possess. Rejection is based on lacking these social credentials. Cliques can create two kinds of pressures: both from belonging and not belonging.

Those *in the clique* can feel socially restricted and confined by similarity demands upon which social belonging depends: "To be in good standing you have to appear like us, behave like us, believe like us, keep up with us, possess like us, only socialize with us, and like us best." For an insider, a clique can be exhausting and oppressive.

Those *not in the clique* can feel rejected and even be mistreated for being different: "To not be one of us means you are not worth noticing and knowing because you don't measure up to us, fit in with us, belong with us, can't keep up with us, and are not as good as us." For an outsider, a clique can be demeaning and intimidating unless one understands that people who group to feel better than others often feel insecure when they can't.

Cliques are close-knit groups in which that closeness is based on required similarity, shunning those who are different, contrasting insiders to outsiders. For example, there can be *wealth cliques* where well-off young people act like they're somehow better, treating lower-income peers as less worthy of consideration, notice, and association.

In the social hierarchy, dominant adolescent cliques can be extremely powerful, sometimes to the frustration of parents and even teachers. Often small, cliques can exercise outsized influence when nonmembers defer to their position. For example, many years ago, before private practice, I was called in to consult with counselors in a middle school over an eighth-grade performance problem. It seemed that an older clique of students who scorned school achievement had gathered so much ruling power that academic effort by nonmember students was actually suppressed. There was among young people who didn't want to offend these influential peers a widespread fear of making better than Cs. So, with counselors, working one capable student at time, we began doing short check-ins with affected students to talk about "not doing one's best," "obligation to oneself," and "braving disapproval." There was no intent to harm the clique, only to honor individual capacity. Gradually the oppressive norm lost its power.

For the middle school moment, being part of a clique can provide some powerful benefits. However, as a larger, more complex adolescent world develops in high school and the reality of senior graduation approaches, the social shelter, simplicity, and similarity of a clique become less serviceable. Now, as conformity demands feel too restrictive, the costs outweigh the benefits, and active membership usually declines.

Eventually, the emphasis on exclusivity is the clique's undoing. By keeping the larger world out, by restricting membership, by demanding conformity of conduct, association, and belief, cliques limit the social path a growing adolescent can follow. What helped at first now becomes more of a hindrance: "I used to run with that group until it started holding me back." ●

Chapter Eleven

Association and Mistreatment

● ● ●

"Why do some people act so mean?"

As freedom of association with peers to form a family of friends becomes more important in middle school, the potential for abusing that freedom also increases in the form of *social cruelty*—mean treatment that young people can engage in and experience with each other as they jockey for social standing and belonging.

This is not to suggest that every middle school student will perpetrate, receive, or even witness socially cruel actions from peers, but it is to say that *five kinds of social mistreatment* do increase during the early secondary school years:

- **Teasing** to put down
- **Excluding** to keep out
- **Bullying** to push around

- **Rumoring** to attack standing
- **Ganging up** to crowd and outnumber

Each of these five actions is intended to victimize, isolate, or otherwise make the target person suffer and feel unsafe and to make the perpetrator feel more socially out of the line of fire or more powerful. Middle school is simply a more push-and-shove age, as young adolescents jockey for social place, belonging, and dominance. Social cruelty is when this push-and-shove becomes abusive, when the intent is its harmful effect.

Why Middle School Mistreatment?

Why associate these damaging behaviors with middle school? For me, the answer is that by middle school, most young people have entered the transforming adolescent passage that begins the awkward process of growing up. In more detail, the following three growth changes have usually occurred:

- They have separated themselves from childhood, no longer wanting to be defined and treated as just a little child anymore.
- They feel developmentally insecure on this account and are more needful of a like-changing family of friends for social support.
- They have begun the physical alterations of puberty, and are more self-conscious and sensitive about changes they cannot control.

Middle school thus captures young people at a more insecure and vulnerable age, when a little hurtful social treatment can cause a lot of personal suffering: "Someone made fun of my play in gym today and everybody laughed!" Public humiliation and social shaming isolate like nothing else.

Five Tactics of Social Cruelty

Consider five common acts of social cruelty and the scary power of each for their target of mistreatment.

- **Teasing** humiliates with insults. It plays on the fear of being inferior: "There's something wrong with me."
- **Exclusion** shuns with rejection. It plays on the fear of isolation: "I have no friends to hang out with."
- **Bullying** intimidates with threatened or actual harm. It plays on the fear of helplessness: "I won't be able to stand up for myself."
- **Rumoring** slanders with confidential truths or outright lies. It plays on the fear of defamation: "I can't stop what is said against me."
- **Ganging up** pits the many against the individual. "It plays on the fear of harassment: "They all join up against me."

What Teachers Can Say

Unhappily, at this impressionable age, now equals later. If adults teach nothing to the contrary and social cruelty is allowed to rule, young people can learn formative lessons about social mistreatment and themselves that can have harmful, larger, and lasting social effects later.

Happily, in each classroom a teacher can moderate this outcome by talking with students about the norm of positive social treatment and communication with each other that is expected in her or his instructional space. When every teacher takes a specific stand for affirmative social conduct, this concerted instruction can have widespread and formative effect. For example, each teacher can communicate expectations.

- **Teasing** can teach social labeling and prejudice through the use of ridicule and name-calling. To counter this, a teacher might say, "In my classroom, I expect you to only call people as they want to be called. You will not make fun of people with put-downs to hurt their feelings."

- **Exclusion** can teach social bias and discrimination through the use of refusing membership and denying association. To counter this, a teacher might say, "In my classroom, I expect that if you see someone being left out or sitting alone, you will invite them to join you. You will not reject people or try to keep them out."

- **Bullying** can teach social harassment and coercion through the use of possible or actual acts of harm. To counter this, a teacher might say, "In my classroom, I expect that no one will push anyone around. You will not threaten or coerce to make a person feel frightened and give way."

- **Rumoring** can teach social defamation and libeling through the use of smears and lies. To counter this, a teacher might say, "In my classroom, if mean gossip comes your way, I expect you not to pass it on. You will not tell stories about people that you know could be hurtful if believed."

- **Ganging up** can teach social persecution through the use of domination and might. To counter this, a teacher might say, "In my classroom, there will be no ganging up to pick on anyone. You will not mistreat any person by using greater numbers against them."

How do teachers explain all this to students? One way is as follows: "Because every act of social cruelty only makes school a more unsafe place to be, don't look the other way or go along with it. In doing so, you poison the well of social experience for everyone. As for engaging in any of these behaviors, you mistreat not only another person but yourself by now acting as a mean person. Thus, by bullying others, you treat yourself as a bully; by spreading lies about someone, you treat yourself as a liar; by following the mean lead of others, you treat yourself as a hanger-on. By treating others well, you treat yourself well."

What Parents Can Say

Parents can also explain about social cruelty: what not to do and what to watch out for should any of these mistreatments come their adolescent's way.

- **Teasing:** People tease to put another person down. They label another person with a name they don't want to be called themselves. It's not about the teased but about the teaser acting mean. *Teasing says more about the teaser than the tormented*

- **Exclusion:** When others don't want adolescents in their group, they can feel rejected, unpopular, and alone. Rather than fault themselves, they should find other friends who welcome their company. *Make exclusion the excluders' loss, not one's own.*

- **Bullying:** People can coerce for dominance. To succeed, they need the bullied to give way. Middle schoolers should try standing up for themselves by refusing to be pushed around. Bullies often stop pushing when the target pushes back. *Braving bullies takes courage.*

- **Rumoring:** Offline and online, people can spread negative or false information to harm someone's social image. People discredit another to make themselves look better. Adolescents need to learn not to argue back, just state the truth. *No one controls their own reputation.*

- **Ganging up:** People use greater numbers to harass some individual or smaller group. Sometimes victims have to reach for higher or outside powers on their side like school authorities or parents to stop mistreatment. *Individual rights deserve protection.*

For parents, the most important support to give to a young target of social cruelty or social inequity (even before addressing how one might stop the destructive behavior) is their important perspective: "Don't believe this mistreatment is deserved or take the mistreatment personally. Don't allow it to injure or diminish your self-worth. Don't blame yourself!"

A powerful example of this learning was reported at a talk I gave many years ago to a local meeting of the Little People of America (an association of people with dwarfism in their families). A mom told how her dwarfed son recounted his middle school days, being name-called about his small size. She got teary-eyed hearing about the teasing he received. That's when her son looked concerned: "Mom, why are you crying?" he asked. "It's so hard to hear about you being hurt so," she explained. That's when her son did a marvelous thing: he smiled and said, "Oh, Mom, their teasing isn't about anything the matter with me. It's about something wrong with them, with what they're doing."

For this young person, knowing not to take social mistreatment personally was a saving grace. Also, by receiving emotional support from a trusted adult, like his parent in this case, his mother provided essential backup at home.

Tough Talking

One byproduct of functioning in a more insecure, push-and-shove age is a harsher use of language with each other to convey a more aggressive social presence—"tough talking," I call it.

Contrasted with childhood, and even early adolescence (ages nine to thirteen), one of the social hallmarks of mid-adolescence (ages thirteen to fifteen) that many parents notice with disfavor is how verbal communication among peers often changes for the worse.

Both offline and online, interaction between their adolescent and peers can become more harsh and slang-ridden. When used by one young person against another, the person roughly spoken to can find it easy to respond in kind. Thus tough talking can be catching.

"Hey, Jerk!"

"Yeah, Ugly?"

And so the game of exchanging insults commences.

Thus, at a meeting with middle school parents, the adult concern was stated like this: "Would you please speak to the 'adolescent culture' of sarcasm, put-downs, labeling, and jokes about one another's bodies, sexuality, and sexual aggression? What is crossing the line these days, and when should a parent step in with their own child and what should they talk about?"

The developmental insecurity that comes with mid-adolescence can have a lot to answer for.

At this juncture, verbal communication can become aggressively protective, even among good friends who find themselves more on guard—even with each other. So, as the parent observed,

- There can be more sarcasm as words are wielded as weapons in an ongoing verbal contest for social dominance: "You dress so last year!"
- There can be more jokes made about others' looks as people are more concerned about their own. "Look at Rughead!"

- There can be more comments about being unwomanly or being unmanly to protect one's own sexual insecurity: "It's Small Stuff!"
- There can be more hostile talk to boost one's reputation through boasting and asserting social dominance: "Out of the way, Stupid!"

In a variety of ways, tough talking can mark the social entry into adolescence, into that more push-and-shove world when one is expected to act more socially aggressive to establish and hold one's place. Offensive, insulting, challenging, or mocking, such name-calling "toughens" interactions up in a larger world where speaking strongly is partly treated as protection against vulnerability.

At the least, parents need to communicate that tough talking to family at home is not okay. So with the middle school parents, we came up with a parental position statement that read like this: "I understand that this is the kind of language you and your crowd at school sometimes use with each other, but it is not okay to use at home among family. It can hurt feelings and discourage safe communication. And just for you to keep in mind: use it among close friends, and the same unhappy outcomes are likely to occur. You can become guarded and less trusting with each other. Tough talking can be costly this way."

The most widespread case of tough talking I ever saw was years ago when, consulting with Central Texas public schools, another consultant and I were called on to intervene in a very small, rural K–12 campus. Here, tough talking that began in the sixth-grade class had spread down into the earlier grades and then up through high school. The students had sufficiently poisoned the well of their relationships with tough talking such that it felt like everyone was either into verbal aggression or was on guard against it.

The message from the principal was, "Most of the students are doing it to each other to keep from getting hurt, and they've lost the old closeness they used to enjoy with each other. What can we do?"

My colleague and I met with the sixth- through twelfth-graders in the gymnasium and helped them talk about what had been going on and why and how it felt, and how by stopping certain kinds of communication and starting others they might recover the quality of relationships with each other that they were missing. Since tough talking was a choice they were making, they could choose to communicate differently if they wanted to. So with practice they did, and as more sensitive and respectful communication began to take hold in the upper grades, it began catching back on in the lower grades as well.

Around the middle school years, peer groups can be socially influential as the push-and-shove helps toughen up young adolescents by their practicing speaking up, standing up for themselves, and give-and-take. At this more aggressive age, it's also important that they treat each other well. Parents don't want them to be either on the giving or receiving end of social cruelty, nor do they want tough talking to be the only way that they converse.

Chapter Twelve

Association and Attachment

● ● ●

"Friends are my home away from home."

I't's hard to socially separate for more independence from family unless one has another social place to belong, with folks similar to you in ways that parents are not—like in age and interests—to hang with and share adventures, to practice give-and-take, and to rely on for an understanding that parents seem too removed to give.

As friendships become more powerful, the possibility of more intimate and romantic attachments begins. Consider the power of best friendship, and then the adolescent crush.

Best Friendship

Most young people instinctively know that their passage through adolescence is no time to go it alone. They need the company of peers who are all struggling with becoming different the same way they are. The most supportive company is to have a best friend—a deeply trusted, highly compatible companion who knows you as well as you do. On the one hand, this intimate connection is extremely positive when given; on the other hand, it can be extremely painful when taken away.

Such a loss commonly occurs toward the end of middle school or early high school. Two young people who believe they are best friends forever (BFFs) are broken apart when one party decides it's time to socially move on, leaving the other behind and alone.

Now the initiating party can feel blamed and guilty while the reacting party can feel rejected and bereft. When parents have a teenager in the rejected role, they need to pay particular attention. What follows is one explanation of common dynamics that may be occurring.

A No-Fault Loss

Begin by understanding that the growing apart between the friends is nobody's fault. It is usually caused by the two drives that propel adolescent development— detachment and differentiation from childhood and parents—that now finds another outlet for expression. Each drive can cause a best friendship to end.

- The drive to detach for more freedom of independence can motivate one party to feel trapped in the friendship and want to be let go to have more social room to grow.
- The drive to differentiate to express increased individuality can cause one party to shed the old relationship to seek a different and more socially fitting definition and identity.

Next consider the kind of closeness from intimacy on which a BFF relationship can be based—mostly on shared similarity.

- We spend all our time together.
- We enjoy all the same things.
- We think just alike.
- We feel the same ways.
- We tell each other everything.

Merged into a single social unit and feeling like they share a common identity, when one party leaves the relationship, part of the other person can feel torn away. The pain from loss of the other becomes pain from loss of self.

Two Kinds of Intimacy

Human relationships create a mix of human similarities and differences. If you can picture a relationship as two overlapping circles, like a Venn diagram, the more they overlap, the more similarity they share, and the less room for differences there are. Relationships of a lasting kind must happily accommodate both human similarities and differences—this is how a *mature intimacy* works.

What an adolescent BFF relationship usually has is an *immature intimacy*— where closeness is based mostly on shared similarities. This is why they are so tight at the time and why they fail to last over the long term. For one party, shared similarity proves socially oppressive, not tolerant enough to accept growing diversity.

What can parents supportively do when a BFF relationship breaks up in middle school and their child is in the rejected role? Take the breakup seriously in the following ways.

- **Provide empathetic support.** The teenager feels a great hole has been created in their life and can feel grief-stricken, empty, and aimless. Take the time at whatever time the young person wants to lament the loss and mourn what is missed: "We'll give a listen whenever you want to talk."

- **Provide transitional support.** Offer temporary social companionship, initiating enjoyable activities together, while the young person is wrestling with how it feels to be left lonely and alone: "Hang with us until you make new friends."
- **Provide reengagement support.** Encourage and enable interests, activities, and social associations that will help the young person reengage with her or his life in new and satisfying ways: "You might try this. It could be fun."
- **Provide perspective support.** Tell the young person that recovering from a significant loss of this kind simply takes time. In six months to a year she or he will increasingly be on the road to feeling better as life is redefined and new relationships are found: "The passing of time will ease the pain."
- **Affirm the strength that loss communicates.** To have had a best friendship testifies to your child's capacity for creating a companionship that matters so much. You can honestly say, "Since you had what it takes to form a best friendship, this means you have what it takes to form other close relationships in the years ahead."

Adolescence is emotionally expensive because growing up requires giving up in many painful ways, of which loss of the BFF can be one. However, the other side of loss can be *freedom from old restraints* and the *freedom for new possibilities*. Parents need to encourage engaging with these opportunities where the young person can.

The Crush

To learn about attraction, young people have to start somewhere, and that early introduction often comes in the form of the *adolescent crush*—a mix of fantasy and romance that can be intensely affecting at the time.

A fourteen-year-old boy wrote and described his experience thus: "About a year ago now I developed a crush on a girl in my class who I had very little interaction with whatsoever and throughout this I was hoping to get to know her. . . . I am still enamored with her and it has had a massive impact upon my mood, sleep schedule, and at times dejection." As he faithfully described it, a crush is often not a casual interest. From start to finish, it can be a very impactful experience.

A crush can be a complicated emotional mix to manage. A crush can

- Feel unexpected: "I was caught by surprise."
- Seem a dream come true: "I've found the perfect someone."
- Create an emotional high: "I feel carried away."
- Feel overwhelming: "I can't think of anything else."
- Feel awkward: "I'm all shy and stumble."
- Take courage: "It's scary to care!"
- Be risky: "Suppose they don't feel the same?"
- Be costly: "I don't have time for friends."
- Be embarrassing: "I keep getting teased about it."
- Be threatening: "Suppose it doesn't last?"
- Be long remembered: "I won't forget my first love!"

Why a Crush?

From what I've seen, middle school and early high school is when most adolescent crushes occur. This makes some developmental sense.

- Puberty has awakened physical attraction.
- Acting older has ignited interest in romantic imagining.
- Curiosity seeks to experience greater intimacy in relationships.

Most important, adolescence is a very impressionable age when the commercial media increasingly and convincingly advertise and glamorize youthful images and experiences to aspire to—romantic ideals among them: "I wish I looked this way!" "I want to experience that!"

While the child socially wanted to have play friends, the adolescent is now growing more seriously inclined, interested in finding a special boyfriend or girlfriend to socially pair up with and share a special caring connection. But how would one recognize such a person? The answer is by finding someone who appears to possess the qualities you find ideally attractive.

A crush is a love-at-first-sight kind of experience that tells less about the person beheld than about the beholder. The holder of the crush projects idealized traits on another person whom they often barely know. Then the projector becomes infatuated with the impression of perfection they have created. And now idealization intensifies emotion with a potent mix of excitement at attraction and anxiety over outcome: "I can't get them out of my mind! What now?"

The Reality

Intensely emotional experiences, crushes are made to arouse infatuation. The reason, as mentioned earlier, is that they are based on the lover projecting personal ideals on someone they actually don't know that well. Mostly they have been smitten with their own fantasy imaginings about what that person must be like. Because the image they have idealized often doesn't have a lot to do with the reality of the person to whom they feel so drawn, crushes are deeply felt but superficial attractions, based on a fantasy vision, which is why crushes usually don't last.

Disenchantment sets in when more reality about the love object is discovered ("She's not as perfect as I imagined") or when ideals of the enamored person change ("What I loved about him doesn't impress me anymore").

As actual experience modifies ideal perception, the other person becomes less wonderful than first supposed. For a truly caring relationship to develop from a compelling crush, the romantic fantasy must be let go, so that realistic interest, liking, and acceptance can grow. Sometimes this happens, but I believe it usually does not. Most crushes don't end with a broken heart, but with a disappointed hope, which is loss enough.

Are Crushes of Value?

Many young people have to get a crush on an ideal fantasy before they can experience the reality of actual love. In this way, having a crush can be an important adolescent rite of passage. A few telling comments about crushes come to mind:

"I didn't know that I could fall for someone before."

"A crush can make you feel really good and really bad."

"You don't choose to have a crush. A crush chooses you."

"Just because a crush doesn't last doesn't mean it's not worth having."

In middle school, significant relationships with peers can become more intense. A romantic example of this is the crush. Just because it is superficially based and not lasting does not mean parents should trivialize the experience. Immature love is still love. They should respect how it entrances and wears off and be prepared to provide empathetic support should it come to a seriously unhappy end.

Part Three

• • •

Freedom for Advanced Experimentation

The High School Years

"It's time to act older!"

Let behaving grown up begin!

Entering high school, one gets to see and know upperclassmates who are much more worldly wise than oneself, and watch peers who are pushing to catch up. Consider it this way.

"High school feels like freedom city where you enter far behind, at the freshman starting line, at the beginning with so much life experience on top of you, which so many upper students already have, striving to keep up with everyone else, growing up as fast as you can as soon as you can so you won't look or act dumb, trying your best by trying a lot more than your parents want you to wait until you are older to try, or just never do, but when is old enough when you're only as old as you act, and only really know as much as you experience, so you don't tell them more about what's going on among your friends, who is really doing what with who, not to upset them into asking you worry questions, because you've got your own worries too, trying or not trying a lot because in just four short years you're out of here and need to know what then because your life is going to

take change in a hurry, so you better wise up now, sooner better than later, daring and driving and dating and drugs and doing what's disallowed, doing these and older things as safely as you can because you're not trying to get hurt, just getting in the know, because you're not stupid, of course there are risks and dangers, but that's how life is so deal with it , lots of accidental hurt out there, sometimes learning the hard way from what happens to friends or to you, learning not to do that again, lucky it wasn't worse, thank goodness for close calls and near misses and lucky escapes, learning more about what parents are always preaching about—responsibility, which you keep taking, biting off more of life as they let go, more daring in high school than your parents will ever know, while managing studies and schedule and spending and social life, which isn't easy to do, all the while worrying about what happens after graduation, plan-ning for that, more work or more school or both, glad to finish high school but missing friends you probably won't see again, missing the aggravation of having parents keeping after you every day, missing living in the home you want to leave, miss-ing friends you won't see again, getting ready for your future, thankful and regretful that high school will soon be over, but feeling sad and anxious too, facing the ever exciting and always scary question: 'What comes next?'"

Well, maybe that's an exaggeration, but on some days not so much.

The pressure to have more grown-up experiences and adventures comes with the high school territory and thus is part of the parenting territory as well, bringing with it the founding instinct to hold on and shield one's child from harm. The world is a dangerous place for the inexperienced, ignorant, and innocent, so parents may get into warning mode to protect by keeping danger away—what not to do and try. But what frightens parents often fascinates their teenager, ready to be let go. There is the excitement: "What an adventure!" There is the promise: "I'll be careful!" There is the hope: "Harm won't happen to me." And there is the reality: "It could." So discussion about understanding and managing the dangers is worth having.

Dire Risks of Adolescence

It is much scarier parenting an adolescent than parenting a child because now the young person is focusing on riskier behaviors, often in the persuasive company of peers, away from parental control and out in the world, more vulnerable to significant harm should things go wrong.

I believe parents should speak to their teenager about *nine dire risks* that can threaten adolescent lives. Over the years, I've seen teenagers fall casualty to each:

- **Social violence:** when aggressive interactions get out of hand
- **Accidental injury:** when unlooked-for dangers suddenly occur
- **School failure:** when educational effort ceases to matter
- **Illegal activities:** when breaking the law feels smart to do
- **Sexual misadventures:** when desire dictates harmful action
- **Suicidal despondency:** when despair leads to acts of self-harm
- **Social pressure:** when going along feels irresistible
- **Dangerous daring:** when excitement urges foolish risks,

- **Substance use:** when drugs alter sober decision-making
  Parents can explain how if the teenager moderates or elimi-
  nates the last, substance use, the likelihood of the other
  eight goes down. This is why *the safest path through the
  adolescent passage is substance-free.*

Risk-Taking

Operationally, risk-taking is gambling, acting in ways that
take chances with one's well-being, pursuing some allure that
also offers harmful possibilities. In adolescence, there are acts
of intentional and unintentional risk-taking.

Intentional risk-taking is deliberate, choosing a course of
action that may turn out well or badly or a mix of both. Exhilara-
tion calls, danger answers, and hurt happens. Or a lesser risk is
taken—say, by last-minute procrastinating: "I knew going without
sleep would stress me out, but I pulled an all-nighter and made
the deadline. Except afterwards, I was too spent to study for my
other classes, so I fell further behind." He hadn't yet learned how
playing the "put-it-off / pull-it-off" game often proves costly.

Unintentional risk-taking is a function not of intent but of
ignorance. A nervous high school junior, excited by her first invitation to a college party, didn't know that she was putting herself
in harm's way by getting drunk and trusting the older guy she
had casually met who had invited her: "I didn't know this could
happen. He told me afterwards how the sex had been consensual. That's not what I remember, but I don't remember much."
No one had warned her about the drinking/socializing dangers
of college life.

Intentional risk-taking is motivated by interest. When harm
happens it is often seen as a "mistake." *Unintentional risk-taking*

is motivated by ignorance. When harm happens it is often seen as an "accident."

Mistakes and accidents can both be risks-come-true that have important safety lessons to teach. Blaming the teenager is not the answer: "That was a stupid, irresponsible thing to do!" Rather, putting these adversities to educational use is what parents must supportively do by talking these experiences out to capture important education each has to teach:. "Let talk first about how you're feeling, then what happened, and then see if there are any useful lessons to be learned."

In general, parents have two ways to help their teenager cope with foreseen dangers—by offering *protection* and by providing *preparation.* Each has its strengths and limitations. Consider protection first.

Protection

Because protection is against possible dangers, it does arouse fears. The more protections against dangers parents give, the more fear they may instill. It's complicated. A built-in dilemma comes with providing protection—whether sheltering or safeguarding. Because protection imposes limits on experience, it can prevent what there is to learn: "Just stay away from that and you'll be okay." But what if exposure happens and the adolescent can't stay away? Ignorance provides no instruction. While protection can increase security, it doesn't provide safety because preventive measures always justify alarm. Thus new protections provide hard evidence of the dangers lurking outside waiting to enter. Like parents who arm themselves to create security, they never just create safety. They also affirm fears.

Feelings of safety can only exist when there is no felt need for protection. Protection never provides only peace of mind.

While parental prohibitions that are backed by reason can have persuasive value, on some occasions they can backfire. To the adventurous, curious, or rebellious adolescent, prohibitions can seem like invitations to experience the forbidden—dangers that only add the incentive of excitement. Sometimes parents who want to "scare kids straight" with frightening possibilities only end up tempting young people on: "If it's that's bad, it's got to be good!" Fear always has a compelling side—excitement of daring the dangerous: "I couldn't resist the thrill!" Come adolescence, fear can be forbidding and inviting.

Growing up in a ruthlessly market-driven society doesn't help. Thus, when laws and advertisers attach an "adults only" designation to some dangerous recreational activity or use, such a limitation may only tempt underage consumers who are in a hurry to act certifiably more grown up. Prohibitions operate as incentives. "Adults only" activities attract adolescent interest.

However, parental prohibitions can sometimes have protective value when the teenager uses them to justify not going along with peers: "My parents would ground me forever if I did what you are doing." As mentioned earlier, the teenager, not willing to lose face with a personal refusal, may use the protection of parental prohibition when feeling unable to say no on her or his own behalf.

Preparation

Another way to address dangers in the teenager's life is preparation. A problem with preparation is that it implies some level of permission: "Not doing this now doesn't mean you won't ever try it, so we need to talk about managing the dangers before you do." Preparation is educational and treats dangers as challenges to be safely met.

While protection limits exposure and relies on warnings and prohibitions, preparation allows more freedom and relies on instruction and often practice. Thus the parent providing protection may say, "Don't do that," while the parent providing preparation may say, "If you try it, this is a safer way." So with substance use, parents can talk about controlling understanding and speed of use: "Always know what you're using, start low, and go slow," they advise.

Protection instills fears; preparation builds confidence. Both parental responses have to do with risk and danger management. When parents teach their teenager how to drive a car safely, they are providing important risk preparation.

Fearful parents sometimes can have a hard time giving effective preparation when some adolescent danger is at stake. Feeling easily threatened, they can lapse into becoming threatening teachers. For example, consider the father and son who finally decided that the dad was not really cut out to teach the sixteen-year-old a dangerous behavior—how to drive a car. Why?

The answer repeatedly given by unhappy experience was the man's protective reliance on warnings and prohibitions, lapsing into panic when he could not tolerate anxiety at his son's trial-and-error learning, the teenager becoming more nervous and upset in response. Every driving lesson drove them into an unhappy place with each other: "So we decided, and my mom agreed, that she would take over the instruction. She can stay calm and composed while my dad just could not. Both of us getting anxious and angry with each other was just hurting our relationship and getting in the way of what I needed to learn."

Managing the Mix

Of course, protecting and preparing are not an either/or proposition since in many decisions parents require a mix of both—saying no to some activities and explaining how to do others. Go back to the matter of operating an automobile, for example. Parents might give a strong prohibition against texting or substance using while driving, but they may give lengthy training for how to navigate a car through heavy traffic.

One of the hardest dilemmas of parenting a young person through the inevitable dangers of growing up is this: *Should I protect my teenager and perhaps foster anxiety and ignorance, or should I prepare my teenager and perhaps allow permission and risk? What to do?*

Maybe this: provide as much preparation as you can, protect as little as you must, and talk and listen as openly as you are able.

Chapter Thirteen

Experimenting and Curiosity

● ● ●

"If I don't try it, how will I ever know?"

Like all emotions, curiosity has both a helpful and a harmful potential. For example, just as fear can discourage effort, it can also warn of danger; just as anger can impulsively attack, it can also confront mistreatment; just as sadness can be depressing, it can also process loss; just as frustration can breed irritation, it can also identify blockage. So, just as curiosity can endanger, it can also educate, having a lot to teach. Because there is always more about life that one doesn't know than one does, curiosity motivates finding out and creating further understanding. While knowledge can sometimes be dangerous, ignorance can be more so: "I didn't know doing *this* could lead to *that*!"

"Don't be scared," "don't be angry," "don't be sad," "don't be frus-trated," and "don't be curious" are simply misguided pieces of parental advice. The management of emotion is a challenging skill that parents have to teach, and I believe it is nowhere near as complicated as instructing about *curiosity*, which always expresses interest—sometimes in what parents approve of, sometimes in what they do not.

Adolescent Curiosity

To appreciate curiosity as a driving force in adolescence, consider a few of its virtues for growth. Curiosity wonders about the unknown, expresses interest, motivates effort, directs exploration, dares the forbidden, wants to discover, tries to figure out, is creative, is inspired by ignorance, is unconventional, asks questions, experiments, investigates, is observant, is thoughtful, takes chances, is inquisitive, is fascinated, is dissatisfied, is inventive, and inspires learning. What a wonderful thing is curiosity! It partly accounts for the longevity of the human race. In addition, curiosity can sometimes be an antidote to such common human ailments as boredom ("There's nothing to do!"), depression ("There's nothing that matters!"), and anxiety ("There's much I don't know!"). Curiosity directs, energizes, and dares.

Of course, there are long-standing prejudices against curiosity.

Proverbial wisdom warns, "Curiosity killed the cat," advising how misguided fascinations can be fatal. *Biblical wisdom* warns not to eat fruit from the forbidden tree of knowledge because original innocence is lost. *Mythological wisdom* warns how Pandora could not resist opening the box of the unknown, loosing untold evils upon the world. On many fronts, humankind has been advised to be wary of curiosity.

Parental wisdom warns the curious child against playing with fire: "You could get burned!" Or parents warn the tempted adolescent about trying recreational drugs: "You could harm your mind and body!" Curiosity is a risky feeling. At worst, it can do us in. However, human history also testifies to curiosity's contributions. Interest in the unknown motivates exploration and invention, solving of problems and the power of creativity. For cures, improvements, discoveries, and a host of human advances, thank goodness for human curiosity.

So parents are caught in the cleft of youthful curiosity. Between disallowing what can be perilously bad and encouraging what can be beneficially good, they deliberate when to hold on and prohibit, when to let go and permit, when to delay so that preparation can be given: "We can't stop you from trying, but we can talk about how to recognize and minimize the dangers."

Curiosity and Growth

Observing their toddler, parents recognize how curiosity drives early growth: "She wants to taste and touch everything around her!" "Watching what we do, he wants to copy and try it too!" Attentive to risks, parents closely monitor this unbridled inquiry, warning the child away from what has potential to harm but also instructing to moderate the hazards of healthy growth: "Always wear a helmet when riding your bike." "Never check email or text when you drive." "The smartphone is the greatest driving distractor ever invented!"

Compared to the inquisitive toddler, teenage interest is even more intense because adolescence is the age of worldly curiosity. Separating from childhood (around ages nine to thirteen), contending with growing physical and social changes, and eager to explore older life experiences outside the sheltered family circle with like-minded friends, the adolescent can feel overloaded and overstimulated by so much of interest.

Sometimes parents are advised to medicate distracting and disorganizing curiosity, to reduce wandering attention, to moderate indiscriminate interest in everything: "He's a little more lethargic, but at least he's not as scattered and impulsive as he was. Now he can concentrate better on his work." This is to the good, but also perhaps at some cost if, by reducing distractibility, some natural curiosity has also been quelled.

The Internet

Comparable to the industrial revolution in generating major social change, the technological internet revolution has been no less impactful, particularly on adolescent curiosity: "With my computer, I can find out about anything anytime I want to know." The internet satisfies, for better or worse, much adolescent curiosity about life.

Maybe in the parent's youth, when a young person asked an unwelcome question about an older experience, she or he might have been told to "wait until you're more grown up and we'll talk about it then." Gone are those days. Goodbye, postponement. Now youth has immediate, twenty-four-hour access to the internet to satisfy curiosity's call. A Wild West of information, some true and much not, is only a quick click away.

Sometimes parents will decide to limit this exposure by monitoring or restricting internet activity, disabling or forbidding usage on home devices where they don't want the young teenager to go. They do this to protect the daughter or son from what they consider dangerous exposures to all kinds of harmful influences, be they sites that deal with violence, hate, sex, drugging, gambling, dating, lawbreaking, cults, conspiracies, or whatever parents fear.

The internet has immeasurably enlarged the playing field of

growing up, challenging traditional parental oversight in the process. Around middle school is when more worldly curiosity often takes wing, and the internet is where much discovery occurs. Certainly parents can feel free to put any restrictions on internet activity that are consistent with their principles and beliefs. However, at most they only have a measure of local influence since they cannot control their teenager's access and activity on the computer devices of friends or that are available elsewhere.

Better Than Restriction

What's a parent to do? Accept the reality of today's information availability and immediacy. Treat any adolescent online searching or experience that parents find worrisome as an opportunity for discussion and providing education. Matter-of-factly help evaluate whatever the young person is reading or seeing or hearing electronically. And be open to follow wherever the young person's curiosity leads. When an adolescent gains earlier internet access than parents might wish, talking about how to weigh this online exposure and information is important to do.

Their advice might be "While it's tempting to believe content that is given, it's best to evaluate it first. So, let's talk about what you've been shown or told and what there is to watch out for—because every internet site is posted with intent, with an agenda. Therefore, as with all forms or media, always ask yourself, *Why would anyone want to post this information, what am I being asked to believe, what response is wanted from me, and why?*"

Internet Exposures

If an *adult internet exposure* occurs that reveals their young adolescent is watching what parents disapprove of or is forbidden, like pornography on her or his computer for a common example, parents need to first assess their own emotional response. If they feel shocked, horrified, disgusted, or furious and are inclined to act that way, they need to emotionally sober themselves up enough to talk about the experience reasonably and effectively. Allowing fright, criticism, disappointment, or anger to drive their response reduces the likelihood that helpful communication will occur.

A simple rule about confronting a forbidden or unwanted adolescent internet exposure is this: *calming before communication.* Take a break. Take a deep breath. Take yourself to a quiet place. Maybe talk first to a friend. Take a moment to appreciate what you love about your child. Take time to get ready to listen, learn, and talk.

Let worst fears rule and you are liable to let expressing your upset detract from your child's education: "I made my feeling upset the focus of our communication. Instead of talking out and finding out what was experienced and learned, I totally shut him down."

Young viewers need adult help to evaluate their internet experience—to see it for what it is, for what it isn't, and for what it really intends. For example, consider a *pornographic internet exposure,* which is increasingly common by the middle school age. As suggested, I believe it's best to treat an unwanted or disapproved internet exposure as a talking point to open up discussion, not a time to criticize or punish, which will only close down communication.

So, after emotionally collecting yourself, simply declare, "In general, I want us to be able to share about our days in two ways—about our offline day and about our online day as well. Existing in two worlds of experience has made life more complicated for both of us this way, so there is much more to keep up with now. Since you have acted old enough to want to watch this kind of internet offering, I would like you also to act old enough to be willing to discuss it with me as well. I'm not out to change your mind, only to offer my perspective for you to consider."

In this case, what might such a statement of perspective include? First, parents can state how sexual curiosity is normal, just as sexual thoughts and feelings are normal. Declare how the purpose of pornography is to stimulate sexual interest. What pornography does show is naked people having sex, so to that degree it can be visually informative: "I never knew what that looked like before."

Then they can explain how pornography is designed to work, like how it is meant for sexual entertainment, not sexual instruction—to compel interest, not to express accuracy. It is for arousal, not education. It pretends and distorts more than it accurately informs. It portrays sex as for sensual pleasure, not for creating emotional closeness. It makes any kind of sexual treatment look acceptable and ignores abuse. It can make having unprotected sex seem okay. It treats people more like sex objects than human beings. It makes human relationships mostly about sex and little else. It can portray exploitive and harmful sex as normal and consensual. What may look okay may not feel okay. Like graphic violence, pornography is for fantasy, not reality.

Whenever you find an unwanted internet exposure has occurred in your adolescent's life, this is a time to encourage communication, not express criticism or give punitive correction. Parents need to keep adolescent internet life, with all its complexities, open for discussion all the time and to share their own growing online experience as well, for good and ill.

Moreover, for adolescents drawn to find out about worldly experience, online life is irresistible. The internet, virtual reality, gaming, and social media have unleashed an evolutionary burst of human creativity, breaking historical bounds. Enthusiastic young people often lead the exciting way to the cutting edge of this technological change. To some degree lagging behind, parents can sometimes have mixed feelings—wanting their teenager to keep up with emerging possibilities while also worrying about the risks of harm. What to do?

In advanced cases, what can work best is treating one's adventurous adolescent as an instructor: "You are learning so much that I don't know. Could you sometimes take me along? Would you teach me what I can't appreciate and don't understand?" Becoming an informed teenage teacher of ignorant parents can be an esteem-filling role.

Then there is the influence of the COVID-19 pandemic that socially quarantined young people or protectively curtailed their physical freedom. One impact has been to make young people even more firmly wed to their online world. "If I can't get out and away offline, then I'll do more exploring online." As quarantine and social isolation diminished chances for real-world experience, reliance on virtual experience has increased.

Curiosity and Risk-Taking

Operationally, *adventurous curiosity* can encourage gambling, acting in ways that take chances with one's well-being, pursuing some allure like excitement that also offers risky possibilities. Sometimes denial is encouraged: "I don't think about the danger, just the fun!" Imagine four high-school friends are caught late at night skateboarding in a deserted downtown parking garage after one crashes and an emergency medical response is needed. What's the appeal of such an adventure? Consider three:

- There is *gambling with chance* and the play of luck. "I wanted to see if I could get away with it."

- There is *sensation-seeking* and the stimulation of daring: "I like the feeling of excitement."
- There is *keeping up with friends* and the importance of social belonging: "I wanted to be part of what was happening."

Adolescents are drawn to normal risk-taking on these counts during their coming-of-age passage because there are a lot of new experiences to try, much growing up to do, and relationships with friends to maintain.

Of course, life is a risky business for everyone because chance or luck has a say in everything that happens.

- Chance keeps creating the unexpected.
- The myriad possible outcomes of any situation are beyond our knowing.
- There is infinitely more that people don't control than they do.
- Although dimly lit by hopes and expectations, the future is mostly dark.
- Plan as people may, happenstance plays a major role in what unfolds.

Talking with young people about risk-taking over the years, I've appreciated the power of luck when hearing accounts of dangerous exposures, near misses, and lucky escapes, as well as counseling casualties of chance misadventures—when discussing lessons learned and recovery is the order of the day.

To help their teenager moderate risks, parents can encourage *looking back* at what happened and *looking ahead* at what might happen.

Looking back on past risk-taking, an adolescent can assume *evaluative responsibility* by identifying and owning what went well, what went badly, and what education they want to carry forward from that experience: "I hope I don't get in another situation like that again, but I kept my head and didn't panic. I could have spoken up earlier to help calm feelings down, and I've learned how to be more watchful when our group starts daring each other on."

Faced with possible risk-taking, the young person can take *predictive responsibility* when tempted to try what is new, different, unknown, interesting, exciting, or whatever others are doing. Parents might suggest that the young person take just a few moments, less than a minute, before diving into some adventure to think ahead about some simple *risk-assessment questions*:

- What is rewarding about doing this?
- What are some risks of doing this?
- Are the risks worth the rewards?
- If so, how can I lower the risks?
- If the risks become reality, what is my recovery plan?

Because curiosity arouses interest, because interest leads to action, because action creates risks, it's best to undertake new experience mindfully. Suggest to your adolescent to take upon themself both evaluative and predictive responsibility. Risk-taking dramatically increases during the high school years when, particularly in the company of friends, experimentation with more worldly experience is on the rise.

Be particularly wary when the teenager is talking in a risk-blind way, in the language of *denial*: "It can't hurt!" "It might happen, but it's not so bad!" "It's bad, but it won't happen to me!" Denial of risks enables injury when a young person doesn't exercise precaution or take preventive action. Now there is reduced defense against possible danger—for example, when driving with seat belts not secured, or when substance sobriety is not maintained, or when texting distracts from driving attention. Pleads the parent, "If you won't do these for you, please do them for me: buckle up, stay sober, and don't be on your smartphone when you drive."

If it's any comfort to parents, from what I've seen, adolescents are curious about far more than they ever actually experiment with. Also, they learn a lot from each other's adventures without adventuring themselves. Not only that, but in the interest of acting older they experiment with a lot of activities that meet with parental approval. Think of beginning employment, skill development, volunteer service, social activism, and preparing for the future. It's hard to think of a young person learning to make their way in the world without depending on healthy curiosity and the willingness to experiment— trying out possibilities to figure out what that way will be. However, curiosity needs to proceed with caution. One aspect of this protective oversight is sensing what one cannot reasonably know: *the protective power of intuition.*

Intuition

A teenage daughter wanted her mother to understand: "Mom, you never even met my new friend before tonight, so how could you know she had a dangerous side?" "To be honest," replied the mom, "I didn't know in the ordinary way of having evidence. I just sensed something reckless about her and felt you should be told, and so I did. I wanted you to be on your guard, that's all."

"Well, you were right. I didn't go along with what she wanted. But others did and now they're sorry. Except for your warning, I'd be sorry too."

What's going on here?

Talking with a parent group a while back, a mother shared words she gave her daughter who was entering high school: "Listen to your instincts. Even though you may not know if what you sense is true, pay it attention. Call it intuition. It isn't always right, but a lot of time it's a sense worth attending to, another way of knowing you can trust."

I believe the mother was giving her daughter good advice. All adolescents are at constant risk because coming-of-age is about taking chances, experimenting and exploring the unknown, undertaking adventures, following one's exciting way in the company of eager friends, constantly playing the lottery of luck. In this journey of growing up, awareness of others and surroundings is always worth keeping, even if the sense or impression or feeling is hard to pin down. Consider it this way.

Suppose that there is *reasonable knowing* based on data gathering and observation that builds persuasive understanding, and that there is *intuitive knowing* based on sensing the desirability or danger of a situation or relationship or opportunity, when there is nothing specific to back it up, at least in the moment.

Reasonable knowing requires some analysis and can be backed up with firm evidence; intuitive knowing is more mysterious and must be taken on trust. People vary in how reasonably knowing and how intuitively knowing they are; most people are a mix of the two. At the extremes, some only make decisions after gathering convincing facts and information; others only proceed when a felt sense of sureness has been reached.

Intuition can pick up on early warning signs before much gathering of information has occurred, such as happened with the mom who advised her teenage daughter. Both kinds of knowing can prove to be wrong, but also at times correct. However, one advantage of intuition is that it often weighs reality before one has had much chance to gather information to evaluate it. Intuition, in this sense, provides *advanced notice* that allows someone to consider a choice before informational knowing has had a chance to present evidence.

- "I avoided trouble by crediting what my senses were telling me."
- "I just felt nervous about going without knowing exactly why."
- "I could just tell the fun would go wrong. I don't know how."
- "Suspicion told me felt I shouldn't trust him, so I kept my distance."
- "Despite how nice she was to me, something told me she wasn't for me."
- "Nothing I could put my finger on, but I decided to leave while I still could."

Mostly people rely on informational knowing for assessing risk and danger, perhaps ignoring intuitive knowing because it is harder to substantiate. However, if in any situation or relationship, without actually knowing why, a young person feels vaguely uneasy, distrustful, suspicious, threatened, anxious, or unsafe, but doesn't know exactly why, that may be a time to credit what one senses and act accordingly.

The power of intuition is that it can provide *prior knowing*. Sometimes, during the chancy adolescent passage, it's better to heed an instinctive sense of warning than to delay and risk painful confirmation later. Or sometimes, when reason cannot make up one's mind, maybe intuition can find the wisest way: "This feels like what is best to do."

When it comes to risk-taking, the parental message might be "If you don't 'know' why, but it doesn't 'feel' right or wise, don't do it." Intuition can have protective value.

High-Risk Takers

Some young people seem to be wired to take high risks. They love the combination of creating challenge, testing limits, braving fear, focusing concentration, living in the moment, seeking excitement, dancing with danger, breaking convention, trying the forbidden, satisfying curiosity, and letting adventurous impulse rule. In these ways, they give themselves more freedom than most of their peers: "She dares to do anything!"

How should parents of such a teen react? With such an adventurous adolescent, when "Don't do it" won't prevent, then "What did you learn from doing it?" must suffice. So the teenager explains, "When night climbing a construction scaffolding, just watch your step, hold on tightly with your hands, and don't look down." To avoid their disapproval, most parents of high-risk-taking teenagers are not told about all the daring that takes place. In such cases, maybe such adult ignorance is merciful. ●

Chapter Fourteen

Experimenting with Dating

● ● ●

"It's time to start going out."

High school dating has a lot to teach.

Is it normal to date in high school? Yes. Is it normal *not* to date in high school? Yes. Which is best? Neither. Readiness to date varies enormously, and this variation should be respected. Timing is a matter of personal comfort.

While dating can bring the enjoyment of acting older and more intense social knowing, it can also create pressure ("What do I wear?" "What do I say?" "What will we do?"). And when any degree of romantic attraction is aroused by steady dating, it can create common questions and concerns, such as

- "How much time should we spend together and apart?"
- "How casual or how serious should we treat the relationship?"

• "How honest should I be about how I feel and what I want?"

Rewarding as it can be, dating in high school is challenging. It demands interpersonal risk-taking and coping with some emotional discomfort. In this sense, nondaters who only hang out with friends for company in high school often lead simpler and less stressful social lives.

Dating Is Serious

Sometimes parents dismiss adolescent dating: "It's not serious." I disagree, because it's formative. Even casual dating is a practice exercise in how to conduct social coupling—how to treat the other person and how to be treated in an attracted couple relationship.

Significant decisions are constantly being made: "When she criticized my inexperience, I kept apologizing." "When he wouldn't stop, I gave in." By the same token, a romantic breakup can leave both ex-partners better prepared for the next caring relationship: "Even though we didn't see a future together, we treated each other well, so that was good."

Dating is a process of approximation as young people learn important social coupling skills that bear on how they will enter a significant partnership later, which young people are increasingly likely to do in the young adult years—around ages twenty-three to thirty.

A Dating Checklist

Parents can offer the teenager a quick checklist for assessing the treatment given and received between the couple. In a healthy dating relationship, the young person should be able to answer "yes" to some basic treatment questions. If a "no" comes up, that means conduct of the relationship and communication within it need work.

- "Do I like how I treat myself in the relationship? Am I a person of equal worth?"
- "Do I like how I treat the other person in the relationship? Do I listen to what she or he has to say?"
- "Do I like how the other person treats themself in the relationship? Do they admit mistakes?"
- "Do I like how the other person treats me in the relationship? Does the person respect my needs and limits?"

Parents should treat adolescent dating seriously because the experience is educational. They should observe what lessons the young person seems to be learning, recognizing the good and suggesting those that might risk harm. Among these is for the adolescent to remember that when navigating the complexity of dating, to help keep it safe, it's always best to keep it substance-free.

First-Love Relationships

I believe most high school students don't experience true falling in love, and when they do, most high school sweethearts don't end up getting married. However, some important lessons learned early about managing a loving relationship can support committed relationships later. A first love is formative when it teaches how there is no free love because getting along requires *compromise*.

Consider how all committed relationships provide some mix of three factors that each party must continually manage.

- There are some *benefits* one seeks—interpersonal rewards in the relationship that provide pleasure and fulfillment in the companionship, both from what one wants to give and get. For example, there is the enjoyment of intimacy from giving and receiving a supportive listen. *In love, there is benefit not only in receiving, but in giving as well.*

• There are some *limits* one accepts—personal freedoms each person is willing to give up in the form of obligations and responsibilities in the relationship, from what one must and must not do. For example, each sacrifices some self-interest to make room for what the other needs. *Loving one another requires making some sacrifice for each other.*

• There are some *risks* one endures—injuries and offenses each person receives from acts of commission and omission by the other, from what happened or didn't happen. For example, there is forgetting something important or not keeping a promise. *The person we love the most can hurt us the worst.*

The best that the young couple will be able to do is to keep the benefits as high as they can, the costs as moderate as they can, and the risks as low as they can. They must make do with some of each. In this way, young people discover how the lessons of love teach the enormous amount of ongoing effort it takes to maintain a caring relationship that has come to matter so much emotionally.

Getting Along

Differences in characteristics, values, habits, and wants beset every human relationship. Dating couples, no matter how casual or serious, have to work through and around these differences, which in fact is a lot of the work in any dating relationship.

Conflict can result for the couple when both parties agree to disagree over some significant opposition or incompatibility between them. Now the challenge is to bridge this human difference by sensitively communicating with care and without criticism and by using concession and compromise to craft an arrangement that both can support, thus unifying a relationship that has momentarily become divided.

"I don't like going to that kind of party!" "Well, I do!" They are invited or expected to attend as an established couple, so now what? Maybe they treat conflict not as a contest or competition, but as a time for working together as a team. By what *creative problem-solving*, what *communication*, what *compromise*, what *concession*, what *changes*, or by what *combination of all of these* can they craft a solution that supports their ongoing relationship?

Maybe something like this: "We'll go for an hour, we'll hang together, we'll talk to people we like, and we won't get into vaping or smoking or whatever else people are doing. And then we'll leave to go out and eat together. People will understand. They know that as a couple we like special time by ourselves."

For sure, parents should take any teenage breakup of a first-love relationship seriously because that romantic attachment can be so intense. Make sure the jilted party receives sufficient emotional support to talk out the loss (the risk of depression—"I don't know how I'll get on without them!") or not act out in harmful ways (the risk of aggression—"I'll get them back for hurting me this way!"). Because the loss of love can feel so painful, recovering from loss can require emotional support.

Sex

In addition to growing curiosity, love increases the desire for physical intimacy, so if a teenager is in a love relationship, the likelihood that sexual activity will occur is higher. Rather than simply let the *urgency of now* rule, as desire alters mood and mind to reckless effect, best to counsel a teenager on how to *plan* to have sex. In doing so, suggest that three rules of sexual responsibility are kept in place.

- Keep it *sober* by not mixing it with substance use that impairs judgment and empowers impulsivity.
- Keep it *consensual* by honoring the comfort needs of both parties so that neither feels forced or has regrets.
- Keep it *safe* by using protections against disease and pregnancy so that these complications are avoided.

"If you're going to act grown up in this physical way in your relationship, then act grown up by taking these three responsibilities. And please remember, if you found love, you don't necessarily have to have sex; and if you have sex, that doesn't mean you have necessarily found love."

Sexual pressure

Then talk to your daughter or son about social pressures that can complicate sexual decision-making, using the more vulnerable example of the girl for them both to understand. At worst, a girl's testimony might sound something like this:

"You just can't win. I know a lot of girls who have had more sexual experience than I have, but I don't feel right about it for myself so soon. Then some of my friends get after me for not doing it, as though until I've had sex, I'm not really a woman yet. Have a few drinks and get it over with, that's what they say. Or do they just want company in what they wish they hadn't done? I don't know. But it sure is confusing. I'm supposed to look as attractive as I can, but then I have to fight off guys that I've attracted. It's crazy.

"So when a guy starts coming on to me, I tell him 'no' and he usually

accepts that and stops pressuring me. But afterwards, in a lot of cases, he doesn't ask me out again, which says a lot about why he wanted to go out with me in the first place. I like being attractive, but I don't like being pressured. And then I get tired from feeling that it's my job to set the limits on how far a guy can go with me.

"Just once I'd like to meet a guy who cared enough for me that he'd want to be careful with me. But you can't trust statements of caring because a lot of times that's just part of their line: using love to make sex okay. It's like a game of conquest to a lot of these guys. And once he wins what he wants, he doesn't want to see you anymore. And you end up feeling used and cheap and angry, and maybe afraid of problems that are your problem now, not his.

"And then there are your parents. They don't understand. At least mine don't. They don't like my seeing one guy too often, afraid I might be getting 'serious,' which is one step closer to having sex as far as they're concerned, and they definitely don't think I'm ready for that. That's why they'd rather I see a lot of different guys—so I won't be in danger of getting involved with any one of them.

"What they don't understand is how dating around can create as many pressures as going with someone. When you date a lot of guys, playing the field can look like playing around. At least that's how people can talk about you, particularly those who don't like you and are just looking for ways to make you look bad. But when you go with only someone, with that time together you get to know and maybe trust each other. Then he's less likely to pressure you in ways you don't like. You don't have to feel hustled all the time, and he's more likely to really care for you so he won't go telling stories about you to his buddies.

"That's what can happen when you refuse to be pressured by a guy you've only dated once or twice. It's not just that he's not interested in *going out with you again. He's angry because you turned him down, because he didn't get to make it with you. So to keep up his reputation he attacks yours. Either he tells other guys that he got me to bed when he didn't, or he'll say he didn't want to with a girl like me because I sleep around with everyone.*

"Then the word gets around that I'm a slut because I'm so easy to get. Of course it's a double standard, because the guys who supposedly slept with me just talk it up like I'm another conquest, which makes them a stud. Well, that's wrong. I think it takes two to make a slut, just like it takes two to make a stud. A girl's no easier to get than the guy who gets her. If it's a conquest, it's as much hers as it is his. At least that's what I believe.

"So here's the deal. *Since harm can happen, I date defensively. Since friends trust and don't play these games with each other, I think it's simplest and safest to just wait and date a friend.*"

When it comes to dating, your teenage daughter is at more risk of sexual pressure than your teenage son, who needs to be specifically told how you expect him to keep any dating experience pressure-free. So you might want to tell your son something like this: "When dating:

"Don't push for physical contact that is not wanted;

"Don't ignore a girl's discomfort or objections;

"Don't blame a girl for turning you on;

"Don't use substances to influence;

"Don't lie to a girl to get your way;

"Don't act sexually entitled;

"Best to date a girl you would like for a friend;

"And treat her respectfully and safely in that friendly way."

Chapter Fifteen

Experimenting and Cheating

● ● ●

"It's not a problem unless you're caught."

Although I believe most parents would counsel their adolescent against cheating in high school as a violation of academic and ethical rules, many self-reported surveys (Google "research on student cheating") suggest that by high school most students have tried cheating at one time or another. It can seem like the easy way to go as it frees you up to get ahead without the study effort. You get around the work demands of adult authority by "outsmarting" it.

However, the regular practice of cheating can prove more expensive than it's initially supposed because, in the larger scheme of things, it encourages the young person to avoid dealing with study demands by getting around them. The explanation that "everybody does it sometimes" is often used to normalize and justify cheating.

Common practice provides social permission for such cheating behaviors as *copying homework* ("borrowing answers"), *sneaking information into tests* ("cheat sheets"), and *plagiarizing content* for one's own ("pirating"). In general, should the school catch a teenager in any of these behaviors, it's best to let the consequences play out: "Now I will be given a zero on the test, and cheating is on my record."

Adolescent rationales can justify these behaviors:

- Cheating is treated as a strategic skill: "It's what you do to get by or get ahead."
- Cheating is about manipulating unfair adult authority: "It's outsmarting the system."
- Cheating is about turning the odds in your favor: "It's how you create your own luck."

Talking About Cheating

How might parents address the issue of cheating with their teenager? Should they say nothing about a behavior that is so commonplace and simply let it go? I think not because the core dynamic in cheating is too serious, too risky, and potentially too formative to ignore. This deception can be destructive because it puts the young person in a false position with themselves and with others, losing trust on both counts: "Others think I know more than I do, while I don't know what I appeared to learn."

Let's consider a young person who effectively cheated his way through high school and is now in college. Now, however, he finds his opportunity for further formal education—which his high grades allowed and ambition wants—blocked by an entry exam where he is to be tested on all the content he was supposed to know. At last, confessing this dilemma to his mom, she didn't criticize his past conduct but simply confronted him with the unhappy reality he now had to face: "I guess you'll have to find some ways to learn the knowledge and skills you cheated yourself out of but that you now actually need—that is, if you are going to get ahead in the way you want." In this case, hard consequences were the best teacher.

Defining Cheating

Further discussion ensued, the mom's concern being about how her son had been mistreating himself and others. Her concern simply put was this: *cheating is lying*. Performance is faked to fool other people into believing one knows more or can do more than is the case. Cheating puts adolescents in a false position with other people and with themselves. It masks a person's true unwillingness or incapacity to perform. Create a regular practice of cheating and the young person risks making a habit of lying to cover up, get by, or get ahead.

Rather than make cheating a conduct issue between parent and teenager, and the young person acting defensively with the adult, I think it works better to treat cheating as a concern for how the adolescent is treating themselves. To do so, parents can first *acknowledge the temptations to cheat* and then *suggest some possible costs*.

Of course, a teenager wouldn't cheat unless some immediate gains came from doing so. Consider a common few: saving time, pretending to know, escaping from effort, fooling the teacher, getting out of work, passing a test, completing a paper, meeting a deadline, outsmarting the system, making a better grade, getting an edge, qualifying, winning, satisfying parents, retaining eligibility, gaining admission, "doing what everybody else does."

There are many motivations to cheat that argue in its favor. By acknowledging these motivations, parents are *not* supporting cheating. They are simply recognizing its many tempting gains. Parents can declare that how much to cheat in school and in life is a matter of choice that people must weigh every step of their way. They can explain, "'How honest do I want to be?' is a question everybody, young and old, asks all the time. 'How much do I want to get away with?' is another. So whether to cheat or not in school is your choice. However, you do need to know that the gains from cheating do not come free."

Maybe the parent also lists some of the common costs: "When you cheat, you don't honestly earn what you get; you cheat on friends who play by the rules; you are being dishonest with others and yourself; you create a false impression of your capacity; you cheat yourself out of learning more; you cheat yourself out of an honest outcome; you create a secret history you don't want others to know; you have something to hide and feel like a phony; you sacrifice honest effort; you choose ignorance in place of knowledge; you corrupt an honor system that depends on truth; you risk facing negative consequences if caught; you live with fear of being found out; you lose trust of others when discovered; you get a reputation for being a cheat; and you may start a cheating habit that is hard to stop. Add up all these and other costs, and the easy way on becomes a harder way to go."

Cheating Is Lying

Then you can reinforce what cheating really is. A credit theft, *cheating is lying*, which is always about illicit freedom—to get away with what's forbidden, to falsify the truth. Because lying creates the need for secrecy from discovery, it estranges relationships with fear of telling the truth and of being found out. It misleads others with untruth who feel betrayed when they find out. I believe no teenage behavior creates more problems for parents than adolescent lying, because in the face of falsehood they don't know what to believe, while the teenager also picks up a load of problems from lying, like undermining the capacity to operate honestly and, when discovered, reducing trust of others in oneself. *Lying cheats about the truth.*

Talk About Lying

When confronting adolescent cheating, treat it as a form of lying and discuss it accordingly. Lying is a kind of storytelling that intentionally covers up the truth with make-believe. The purpose of this falsification is to control the narrative about what did or didn't happen, what is happening, or what will happen. The persuasive power of lies depends on how convincing the storyteller is and how trusting the audience is—how much they want to believe what they are told.

As their prime informant about the adolescent's life, most parents want to trust that their teenager is telling them the truth. Without that trust, they can experience a very painful emotional state: ignorant, angry, and anxious: "We don't know what to believe!" "We feel betrayed!" "We can't trust you!" Lying that works requires collusion between the teller and the told: "We trusted what you told us."

Teenagers seem drawn to lying as a moth is to illumination, only instead of light being the attractor, the allure is freedom because adolescence is a more freedom-loving age. While parents often view lying as a moral issue, to the adolescent it is often just seen as a practical one. Lying is about claiming illicit freedom to get out of trouble or getting to do what is forbidden.

Lying comes in two major forms. *Lying by omission* is deliberately keeping parents ignorant of information they need to stay adequately and accurately informed: "You didn't ask, so I didn't think you wanted to know." The teenager wanted freedom from parental discovery or oversight: "Parents keep best in the dark."

There's also *lying by commission*, which is deliberately misleading parents by falsifying information about what was, is, or will be going on in order to get what is wanted: "I told you there wasn't going to be drinking at the party so you'd let me go." The teenager wanted freedom for some forbidden experience: "Parents mostly know what they are told."

I think that at some points during growing up, all teenagers lie to their parents, and at some point all teenagers get caught. I also believe that at all such points of occurrence, parents should confront adolescent lying. There needs to be discussion that explores how it feels to be lied to and how it feels to lie because lying has powerful emotional consequences on both sides of the relationship: "Not only are you treating us with deception and so injuring our trust in you, you are treating yourself as a deceiver and so injuring self-respect. You are degrading yourself by acting like a person who is unable or unwilling to own up and tell the truth."

When a Lie Is Told

In general, when adolescent lying occurs, parents need to get an explanation of why the lie was told, exact a commitment not to lie again, and apply some specific household consequence to symbolically work off the offense. The last step is the hardest. Although it's easy for parents at this juncture, feeling wounded and betrayed and suspicious, it can feel easy to say, "And it will be a while before you earn back our trust." This position is not workable. First, it places parents in a state of continual distrust, which creates ongoing anxiety;

second, the teenager may well think, *If they're not going to believe me anyway, why tell them the truth?*

Parents must finally declare their ongoing intent to hold the young person to honest account because in healthy human relationships this is what people need to do: "Just as you expect the truth from us, we expect the same from you. No one likes to be lied to. For the liar and the lied to, dishonesty is a harmful way to live."

Habitual Lying

By "habitual lying," I mean when lying becomes a preferred operating style to manipulate and misrepresent reality for the sake of protecting or advancing one's immediate self-interest. Habitual lying commonly becomes a reflexive response to accusation, temptation, or threat. Now there is no sense of obligation or responsibility for accurately or openly portraying what happened, is happening, or what one is intending to have happen. The guiding principle seems to be, "I just make up what I want people, and even me, to believe as I go along." Fiction is presented as fact.

An extreme example of habitual lying during adolescence is when lying becomes an essential habit used to enable substance or other addiction. *Most addiction is partly to lying* itself—to escape discovery by others, to gain repeat access to what one compulsively craves, and to avoid admission about the self-destructive dependency that is ruling one's life. Addictive dependency is easier to get into than out of, and is enabled by deception.

Becoming expert at conning other people and themselves into believing what isn't so, even in support groups and treatment, the addicted adolescent's habit of lying can linger, creating a major resistance factor in recovery and a major risk factor for slips and relapses: "Once I start lying, I'm on my way back to using again."

This is why all recovery from addiction requires the courage to confront, confess, and commit to painful truth. Thus, assisted abstinence programs like Alcoholics Anonymous (AA) and its variants place a premium on truth-telling to self and others and provide support to that end. Inpatient and outpatient treatment programs help young people get honest with themselves and others. Sobriety and recovery depend on developing a new habit—rigorously holding oneself to truthful account.

Of course, getting into a pattern of habitual lying for the freedom-loving adolescent doesn't require addiction. It can begin simply with accomplishing many objectives that are tempting to gain. Consider a few common uses for youthful lying: concealing the truth, exaggerating the truth, creating a false truth, getting ahead, exploiting ignorance, preventing discovery, denying reality, faking what's going on, escaping responsibility, having one's way, or avoiding consequences. Lying is a powerful persuader in so many ways, no wonder it can come into such heavy adolescent use. As with cheating, in the short term one gets ahead, but in the long term reliance on deception has lessened the capacity to operate honestly.

Unhappily, coupled with the teenage temptation to lie is the parental temptation to believe lies the adolescent tells. The concerned parent asks the teenager, "Is everything going okay?" The truthful answer is, "No, a lot is going wrong." But to keep parents in ignorance so they don't interfere, the adolescent lies: "Sure, everything is fine." And because parents don't want their worries aroused or confirmed, they reply, "That's good to know." It's not just tough to tell the truth;

hearing it can be tough also. Parents live in denial when they discount the data and lie to themselves.

Many habitual adolescent liars can be skilled manipulators and charm artists too—easy to believe and easy to forgive on that account: "He's such a good kid. He's so repentant when he gets caught. I feel so sorry for him. I always want to give him the benefit of the doubt and another chance." Probably the most common parental denial of adolescent lying comes in the form of hope—hope that their suspicions are unfounded, hope that what happened before won't happen again, hope that conduct will get better, hope that from now on, truth will be told.

Honest Communication

Part of parenting is preparing a teenager now for self-management later. What the adolescent learns from adult instruction, interaction, and example in family circumstances informs her or his conduct in outside relationships and those to come. Thus, how the adolescent learns to communicate with parents has a bearing on how this young person will communicate with others after leaving their parents' care. Having parents who model and expect honesty is probably best. To get along in later life, it can make a powerful difference if the young person has been taught to be an honest communicator and not a deceptive one, to courageously face the painful truth and not run from it: "Painful truths are hard to tell, but life gets harder when you don't."

Obviously, parents cannot compel a habitual liar to operate on a more truthful basis with them. However, they can choose to confront lies when they are found out and talk about how lying affects caring relationships and how relying on lying to their parents puts the young person at risk of doing so with others later. Parents can itemize some basic costs of deceit by explaining how nothing corrupts caring relationships like lies for these reasons:

- One can't have trust without truth.
- One can't have intimacy without honesty.
- One can't have safety without sincerity.

Parents can talk about the primary objective of lying: to control the narrative about what happened, didn't happen, is happening, and will happen. They can also explain how habitual lying is eventually self-defeating because sooner or later it creates more problems than it solves. As Abraham Lincoln said, "No man has a good enough memory to be a successful liar." It takes lying to cover up lying until at some point liars can feel out of control because they can't keep all their stories straight. They lose track of what they said to cover their tracks, slip up, and get caught—and then earn their reputation for lying. Thus, liars can become their own worst enemy.

Lying is much more labor intensive to manage than truth-telling, because lies require deception. Truth has only one story to remember, but lying always requires remembering at least two: the truth about what actually happened (what not to tell) and the fiction that was made up to conceal the truth (what was told instead). Habitual liars start lying to gain control of their story but increasingly feel a loss of control over all the fabrications they have created, acting like a fugitive and feeling anxious on that account. Habitual lying is a very stressful way to live because it puts the young person in a false position in so many troublesome ways.

This is why, when all is falsely said and done, adolescents who engage in habitual lying end up feeling distant and cut off from family, fearful what closeness might reveal. Many such teenagers are very lonely people because they cannot be their true selves with anyone. How isolating is that? Thus, a young person is often relieved at being caught because now she or he has a chance to get back on an honest footing with those they love. Then they can come out of hiding, and the narrative of their lives becomes simpler to remember and to tell.

Now they can stop feeling fearful of being found out. They don't have to be so vigilant. They can feel more relaxed and connected. They can be truly known, understood, and legitimately trusted.

If parents see their adolescent getting into a pattern of habitual lying to get what is wanted, to get away with what is not allowed, or to get out of what is not wanted, they can explain the human costs of this deception and encourage the harder habit of telling the truth, however painful or scary that might be. *Cheating on the truth is a self-destructive way to grow.*

Chapter Sixteen

Experimenting with Substances

● ● ●

"It's just for the fun of it."

The older one grows through adolescence, the more one wants to act grown up, and the more likely this includes experimenting with substances readily available in our drug-filled world. While the incidence of adolescent drug use increases, particularly in social situations, a significant percentage of young people in high school still elect not yet to use, while more become chemically active after leaving home as social use, ease of access, and the variety of available substances all increase.

Psychoactive Substances

A psychoactive substance is a mood- or mind-altering chemical that is taken to alter one's emotional or conscious state—to help enjoy a good time or to cope with a bad time. By the end of high school, most young people have tried some degree of use of some of the big three: nicotine (a stimulant), alcohol (a depressant), and marijuana (can be experienced as a hallucinogen, a stimulant, or a depressant).

A substance, like any drug, is just a poison with a purpose, always risky because intended good effects can also have unwelcome bad effects, varying from person to person. As such, use of psychoactive substances is always a gamble.

Why Use?

People use for freedom:

- *Freedom for* relaxation, companionship, comfort, confidence, unwinding, release, escape, and fun.
- *Freedom from* stress, suffering, pressure, tension, anxiety, insecurity, self-consciousness, and worry.

Most commonly, I believe young people use recreational drugs to affect their emotional state—to relax tension, to reduce suffering, to elevate mood, to alter perception. So the nature and management of emotion is worth discussing. While emotions are good advisers (part of one's *affective awareness system* that senses when something important is happening in one's inner or outer world of experience), they can be very bad advisers for what to say and how to act. Substance use can intensify emotional influence in a number of harmful ways.

- Drug use can encourage anger and increase aggression.
- Drug use can encourage fear and increase anxiety.
- Drug use can encourage frustration and increase impulse.
- Drug use can encourage desire and increase indulgence.

The more one uses a substance, the less that judgment—and the more that emotion—is likely to influence one's decision-making.

Thinking with one's feelings increasingly takes over. Substance use empowers your emotional side as rational sobriety is lost.

Denial

Denial is *the enemy in hiding from what's in plain sight*: admitting when substance use has become endangering.

- "Everybody does it."
- "I don't have a problem."
- "It won't happen again."
- "It's no big deal."
- "I can handle it."
- "I can quit any time I want."

Why deny? Because protecting one's continued use has now become a priority; preserving the freedom to use matters more than admitting the costs of use. Denial makes it hard to assess one's level of use, and on which substance-using level one is operating. Consider these *six progressively serious levels of use*, from least to most dangerous, that a young person can experience:

Experimental use: Ingesting a substance out of curiosity and deciding not to use it again: "The others were trying it, so to see what it was like, I did too." Although the least dangerous level of use, experimentation is never safe because the outcome (how the drug will affect you) is always a gamble. The danger here is that how you're affected can be unexpected.

Recreational use: Repeatedly using for pleasure socially, in moderation, with no harm done to self or others: "It just eases how I feel, takes the edge off, and relaxes me for fun." This is the most common level of use, and the most likely to be encouraged by experience. The danger here is ignoring what may become an individual or social habit.

Accidental excess: Unknowingly using too much, suffering from unexpected painful consequences, and not repeating them: "One minute I was using as usual, but then I lost it." Unintentional, the danger here is use uninformed by forethought or judicious oversight that in the moment alters one's functioning for the worse.

Intentional excess: Knowingly seeking excess (becoming drunk or wasted) for the sense of freedom that overindulgence can bring: "Keep using and I can act any way I want." Now the substance seems to set its own rules. Intentional, the danger here is acting like there is not enough, so safe limits are very hard to set.

Abusive use: Consumption that often leads to self-endangering or socially harmful behavior under the influence: "Afterwards I have to deal with what I didn't know I was doing or wish I hadn't done." The danger here is how the empowering effects of harmful use can be regretted, but may be insufficient to deter doing so again.

Addictive use: The combination of withdrawal, craving, compulsion, and denial now support a regular dependence on a self-destructive substance to survive: "I know it's bad for me, but if I don't have my usual dose, I'm not okay." The danger here is becoming trapped in a pattern of harmful substance use to organize and support daily life.

While no use is without risk, if your teenager is operating on any of the last three levels, get an outside assessment of the young person's use because these can be gateway motivations leading to damaging involvement.

Suggestions for Safe Use

Parents might want to consider offering their teens the following pieces of advice for relatively safe substance use:

- Make use intentional, not automatic.

- Make use a free personal choice and not socially pressured.
- Don't use to keep up with or compete with other people's use.
- Use in the company of friends, not strangers.
- Use because you want to, not because you need to.
- Whatever you are using, keep the dose low and go slow.
- Know why you are using. Have a reason.
- Plan your use and keep to your plan.
- Don't use and drive and don't be driven by someone using.
- Stick to a single substance when using.
- Use for enjoyment, not to medicate discomfort.
- Use so that, looking back on your use, you have no regrets.
- Curfew your use. Don't use after midnight.
- Don't use to be grown up.
- Afterward, soberly evaluate each episode of use: was it safe?

Essentially, if your teen is going to use substances, try to teach them to keep it safe and enjoyable. An adolescent who can't use without losing rational sobriety to emotional urgency and endangering action needs to modify their use or get help.

If your older adolescent needs help stopping destructive use, there are *assisted abstinence programs*, such as AA or other twelve-step programs, that offer group support for sober living. Outpatient and inpatient treatment programs also provide therapeutic understanding to break free of substance dependency.

Because substance use can easily intensify and disinhibit emotion, the power of maintaining emotional sobriety also counts for a lot when it comes to rational functioning. Keep in mind the growing emotionality of adolescence and how parents can become more emotional in response.

Adolescent Emotionality

As a child grows into adolescence, emotional demands on parents can often increase. Why? The answer is that while it takes a lot of emotional energy to help a child securely attach to parents, it can take even more emotional energy to stay well connected to a teenager once the ten- to twelve-year adolescent transformation gets underway.

Just consider some teenage changes with which parents must contend and some emotional demands on parents while these are unfolding:

- As the young person pushes for more independence, she or he can feel more *frustrated* by parental oversight and restraint; parents can find more active and passive opposition more frustrating when it occurs.
- As the young person expresses more individuality, she or he can feel more *hurt* by parental disapproval and criticism; parents can feel less appreciated when youthful discontent with them occurs.
- As the young person pulls away for more privacy and separation, she or he can feel more distant and *lonely*; parents can feel more removed and disconnected when growing separation occurs.
- As the young person experiments more with the forbidden and unknown, she or he can feel more *anxious* on that account; parents can feel more worried that dangerous and damaging outcomes may occur.
- As the young person acts more resistant to parental governance, she or he can feel *angrier*; parents can feel more resentful when growing challenges to their authority occur.

Because on all counts, parents are now living with a more emotionally intensified adolescent and are at risk of more emotional response than before, modeling their own emotional sobriety and self-management is extremely important. It affects how parents communicate and act, which not only impacts the young person directly, it often encourages them to imitate the example parents set. Having touched on emotional sobriety earlier, it is worthwhile considering it again.

An unhappy example of its loss can be when impatient parents lose their temper and explode, and the teenager feels inclined to do the same, and now both engage in a yelling match in which nothing productive is accomplished and hasty words may inflict hurt. A happier example is when the young adult can look back and appreciate the model they were given: "No matter how upset I was feeling, my parents kept their cool, and that always cooled me down."

So, back to emotional sobriety.

Emotional Sobriety

"Emotional sobriety" refers to the parental capacity, when pressed or challenged in the relationship with their adolescent, to *let judgment, not emotion,* rule. Parents remain

Calm in conflict or crisis. Their voice is not raised.

Caring in conduct and words. They do not become hostile.

Focused on the issue at hand. They do not stray to other issues.

Reasonable in expression. They do not let impulse rule.

Attentive in listening. They do not tune out what they disagree with.

Lose emotional sobriety in the moment, and spoken language can change for the worse in three common ways. Choice of words can change from *objective* ("This is the situation") to *evaluative* ("This was really irresponsible"). Choice of words can change from *moderate* ("This is what can sometimes happen") to *extreme* ("This is what always happens"). Finally, choice of words can change from dealing with the present ("This is what we must deal with now") to dooming the future ("You'll never live this down").

With parents and an adolescent who are caught in a hard place with each other and are emotionally slugging it out in counseling, one helping role is to assist them in restoring more constructive communication with each other. I suggest "let your emotions dictate your language, and your language will only intensify your own and each other's emotion."

It can take a huge amount of self-discipline for parents to retain emotional sobriety with an aggressive or intense adolescent so that better judgment and not impulsive feelings can rule. It often takes more self-discipline to maintain rational self-control when parenting an adolescent than it did parenting a child. ●

Part Four

• • •

Freedom to Claim Emancipation

The College-Age Years

"Now leading my life is up to me!"

Let self-rule begin!

High school over, entry into the larger world creates exciting freedoms and increased demands that at times can feel very challenging to master. Consider it this way:

"Of course this is what I've always wanted or said I wanted, 'Leave me alone,' 'I can handle it,' 'Stop managing me,' what I've been pushing for, being out on my own, away from home, no parents to boss me around, to check and see how I'm doing, free from their watching and control, but I never figured how much work flying solo would be, so much to take care of so much of the time, so much responsibility, worried about getting around to it, because if I don't then it won't get done, that simple, and if I forget I won't be reminded, and when I mess up clean-up is up to me, and what I put off just adds to what needs doing later on, so the pressure won't let up, and while escaping into fun relieves it for a time, when I come back it's waiting for me harder than before, just piled up on other stuff, so now there's more to do, no getting away from work because now I'm in charge, giving the orders, setting the limits, making the rules,

keeping after me to keep after it, but instead of telling my par-
ents, 'You can't make me!' now I'm telling myself 'I can't make
me!' tired of me bossing me around, wanting a break, some
relief, and then there's the future, what I'm going to do with
myself, because the present keeps running forward, while life
doesn't last forever, and you only get one ride, choices now mat-
tering for choices later, and there's good friends out for a good
time, so much stuff to take and play with, slipping and sliding
but they don't care, even crashing, wanting me not to care, and
it's tempting, but the price of playing along can be messing up
for me, so I try to stick to what I know is best, like taking care
of business and working to get ahead and advancing where I
can, keeping after it, not screwing up what I truly care about,
easier to say than do, but if I don't who will, I mean leading my
life is up to me, planning where I can, scrambling when I can't,
building for what I'd like to do, to get, to be, pushing myself to
make and find a better way, when much that happens isn't up
to me, luck calls so many shots, circumstance is never fair, and
when I'm making it some days telling myself, 'Good going!'
then getting back to work because life is a nonstop proposition:
there's always more to do!"

Well, maybe that's an exaggeration, but on some days not so much.

It's time to start making the break from the home and family nest, miss it as one may. No love is lost, but a declaration of independence has been made, and parents must adjust to this new phase in their relationship with the growing older child now acting all grown up, or trying to. At this vulnerable age, the adolescent doesn't need either doubt or criticism from parents, since the challenged young person has enough of both of their own. Rather, she or he needs their expression of faith and confidence. This is not a good time for parents to ask, "What's wrong with you?" after a mistake is made, but rather offer, "Look at all you're doing right!"

The end of adolescence is a very self-absorbing stage of growth, for some young people almost as powerful as the separation from childhood at the beginning: "Becoming my own person is exciting and scary and hard to do. I'm running behind and I need to get better!" Every day can feel like a new audition for independence, trying out for the adult role one is now expected to play. Encountered are many accommodations between what one ideally wants in life and what they can realistically get: "There's a lot of let-down when you finally grow up." Self-appraisal can also take a downward turn: "I'm not as ready as I thought I was." As for parents, they often face some common losses in the process of letting go of their traditional standing in order to stay caringly and communicatively well-connected to their developing, departed child.

The Parental Adjustment

The challenges of parenting never end, thus the question: "Assuming an older adolescent is successfully transitioning into young adulthood, what adjustments might a parent want to make so that closeness with their independent child can continue to grow?"

Consider a number of common adjustments.

Demotion: Parents lose positional superiority. Interpersonal standing is now equitized: "I can't pull rank of ruling authority anymore."

Distance: Parents lose central importance. They become more peripheral to young adult life: "I'm more of an outsider now."

Disappointment: Parental expectations are unmet. Old dreams do not match the emerging reality: "She didn't turn out exactly as ready as we hoped."

Disapproval: Parents may question daily decisions being made. They would choose differently. "We don't agree with all his priorities."

Diversity: Parents feel a loss of similarity. The new lifestyle is increasingly unfamiliar: "Her values are different from ours."

Distance: Parents lose accustomed closeness. Primary intimacy is found elsewhere. "I miss the contact we used to share."

Deprivation: Parents lose current information. They feel more out of touch with what is happening: "I'm told less about what's going on."

Directness: Parents lose spontaneity of communication. Conversations are more measured: "I'm more diplomatic about what I say."

Straining the Relationship

Of course these adjustments are not mandatory. Some parents will object to them, and that may be fine. But consider how the parent/adult child relationship might be strained when such adjustments are declined.

Parents can *resist demotion:* "We're still your parents. You will do as we say."

Parents can *insist on involvement:* "We'll still be an active part of your daily life."

Parents can *express disappointment:* "You're not fulfilling our expectations."

Parents can *become a source of criticism:* "You're making immature decisions."

Parents can *oppose diversity:* "How you live your life is not how we live ours."

Parents can *express despondency:* "We don't know what to do without you."

Parents can *miss intimacy:* "You don't keep us as close as you always have."

Parents can *stick to directness:* "We will continue to speak our mind as always."

Such responses may be okay—but increasingly they may not.

Role Adjustments

Proceeding as though your adult child will lead a family-centered life usually doesn't work too well. Instead, by emphasizing certain parental roles, closeness can continue to grow. Parents can become

- **Cheerleaders,** celebrating accomplishments: "Good for you!"
- **Supporters,** providing empathy: "We're always here to listen!"
- **Motivators,** encouraging effort: "You're making it. Keep on going!"
- **Followers,** expressing interest: "We always want to hear what's happening."
- **Mentors,** advising when asked: "We can share our experience with that."

- **Companions,** providing welcome company: "We love to see you any time!"
- **Independents,** leading separate lives: "While we miss you, our lives carry on."
- **Informants,** sharing home and family news: "This is the latest on the other kids."
- **Helpers,** being on family call. "Always let us know when we can lend a hand."
- **Requestors,** asking for assistance: "Should we have need, we will give you a call."

Now begins a new grown-up living side-by-side with parents as separate individuals, with the parents content to live more on the young adult's terms. For the young person, parents become less of a daily focus, although no less loved. They have simply been moved at a further distance as the more self-absorbed young person places a necessary priority on building and conducting an independent life.

Chapter Seventeen

Emancipation and Preparedness

● ● ●

"I'm not as ready as I thought I'd be."

The endgame of parenting a high school senior can be complicated. Whether she is soon to be living at home on more independent terms, leaving for a job and apartment-sharing, or moving on for further schooling, a forthcoming change in their relationship is underway. At this juncture, parent and adolescent may have very different views of how to proceed with the impending separation. Getting ready to leave home in one way or another is a big deal for everyone: high school graduation can be an affirming ending, a sad goodbye, and a worrisome beginning.

For the young person leaving, this departure can feel like saying farewell to a lot of precious history with old friends—senior year is a hard letting-go—while anxiously preparing for more freedom and independence and the unknowns that lay ahead. For the parents being left, there is a lot to miss that they will never have again. It is the end of one family era and the beginning of another when their teenager grows more apart and parents become more socially peripheral in the young person's life.

Adolescence is bounded by two losses for parents: the separation from childhood at the beginning and the empty nest at the end. Now, just as the adolescent has a lot to take on, parents have a lot to let go. Everyone is challenged by the change.

Transition points in human life are hotbeds for ambivalence—wanting and not wanting to let go of what is old and familiar, wanting and not wanting what is new and different. At this point, the young person may echo a memorable youthful sentiment about parents: "I don't need them now, except when I still do." So the young person wants it both ways: to be let go without interference, but also to be held on to with support should the need arise.

Senior-Year Mismatch

In some cases a mismatch can occur during the teenager's senior year, that jumping-off place when planning for some degree of leaving family is underway. At this delicate departure point, while parents are focused on the young person's readiness and enjoying diminishing precious time with them at home, for the older teenager his or her parents' needs and well-being may be the last thing in mind.

While parents may be struggling with impending loss and are wishful for a sweet departure time together, the teenager is beset with concerns about moving on and so can be more unavailable, impatient, and unmindful of them. While parents may want some good family time together, the teenager may want more time to be left alone at home or socially with friends: "I've got a lot on my mind!" And now there can be more bickering with each other: "We need to talk with you about your plans for what comes next!" "Not right now! Can't you see I'm busy?" Departure anxiety is at work.

Parents can wonder why they're treated more impatiently. Consider some possible explanations.

- The young person is socially starting to leave home while still living there to make the coming separation easier to bear.

- The young person alternately giving them static or silence is not meant to trouble them, but rather expresses her or his troubled state.

- The young person is distancing and dismissive with parents to mask unreadiness anxiety about leaving that she or he doesn't want them to know.

- Treating parents with apparent inconsideration, the young person is taking for granted trust that no matter what, the parents will always be there with love and support.

- The young person is so intent on keeping their outside world together and preparing for the future that coming home there's not much effort left for parents.

- By disengaging from parents the young person is trying to show she or he can live more independently of parents while still living at home.

- The young person is truly mixed about wanting and not wanting to leave home and is acting out this discomfort with parents.

- In the young person's reluctance to leave, she or he is acting in unwelcome ways in the hopes parents will urge them out, even act happy to see them go.

- The explanation I find most likely is that the young person is so self-preoccupied at this major transition point that she or he is truly insensitive to what this hard time is like for parents, unmindful of their needs.

Usually betting on this last explanation, I suggest that parents ask for what they need: "We know you have a lot on your mind right now, but we would love to have some good times with you before you leave and to be treated not as being in your way but here to help at this challenging time. Can we talk about how to do this?"

Senioritis

A sign of unreadiness is commonly called "senioritis"—an academic letdown in the final year of high school. Quite common, there can be a reduction of study effort by some students in high school as graduation looms into view, particularly in the final semester. Now doing work seems to have given way to letting up as the finish line draws near. For some students, the desire to keep working can become less easy to maintain.

I believe that senioritis is a mix of fatigue, loss, anxiety, and escape.

- **The fatigue** can be weariness of schooling that sets in as the end of high school approaches, particularly if preceded by a strenuous junior year spent working extra hard to boost academic standing for college admission's sake: "I'm tired of the grind. I want to give myself a break. Now grades don't matter anymore."

- **The loss** can be starting to miss the circle of peers that has socially defined and enriched their lives these many years, companionship soon to be lost after graduation when everyone goes their separate ways. Senior year can turn into one long social goodbye: "I'm going to miss our hanging out. I want to spend this final time with friends."

- **The anxiety** can be facing the reality of jumping off into an unfamiliar and uncertain future after high school and worrying about so much that is unknown: "I don't feel ready for this next step. I'm not sure I can make it. Suppose I lose my footing or can't find my way?"

- **The escape** can be disengaging from dedication as more responsibility is soon to be required, letting up on effort as more effort is soon to be demanded, focusing on the present to avoid dwelling on the future: "I just want freedom from all the work the next step is going to take."

Graduation Ambivalence

In addition, at an age when they are fast becoming their own ruling authority, students have met the enemy, and it is them. *Soon it will be my job to make myself do the work!* Beset by their own resistance to moving forward in life as the last year in high school winds down, the enemy can also be *ambivalence*—wanting and not wanting to graduate, wanting and not wanting to act more independently, wanting and not wanting to move on. This ambivalence can make their current attitude toward work extremely discomforting for parents. Rather than fight adolescent ambivalence and in doing so often intensify it, it is usually better to talk about the mixed feelings, accept them, and then encourage effort at a time when making that effort can feel harder to do.

Continual Effort Counts

It's easier to opt out of a grind and experience relief than to get back into a routine and face those old familiar pressures, just like taking vacation is easier than returning to work. Parents can suggest to a student falling victim to senioritis, particularly one who is college bound, that students who graduate high school still working hard tend to be better prepared for the rigors of college study compared with those students who have let effort go during senior year. Better for the college bound to treat senior year in high school as preparation and conditioning for freshman year in college by keeping up the academic effort. Even if otherwise employed and living more independently, staying in working form definitely helps. Whatever their next step after high school, it will take strength of self-discipline to meet the challenge.

Sometimes lapsing students will feel disappointed in themselves and fearful for themselves when their traditional will to work has become momentarily disabled: "I'm letting myself down!" "Suppose I don't get myself going again!" Knowing they are acting in a self-defeating manner against their own better interests can cause young people to wonder if they are mentally okay. In response, it's usually best for parents to explain how senioritis is not some kind of psychological disorder or disease; rather, it is a common response to the complexity of finishing high school, often partly rooted in ambivalence about moving on.

At home, parents can recognize and normalize this frustrating state, encouraging the young person to talk about it and giving an empathetic listen, all while encouraging and recognizing efforts that enable successful engagement and getting ready for the next working step to more independence.

Assuming functional independence is highly demanding. Going off to college, for example, requires much more than simply meeting a new set of academic demands. It takes a lot of work on many fronts, *work being the process of investing effort in a task to achieve some desired or demanded outcome.*

Part of what the entering freshman needs is a readiness for work to help them catch their footing in college. And as any college will tell you, the retention and graduation rates don't lie: this transition is hard for many young people to make right away out of high school.

If you don't believe me, ask your college of choice about their *freshman retention rate*: what percentage of first-year students don't return sophomore year? Of those who do return, what percentage graduate in four years, in five years, or fail to graduate at all? Since every college has this data, ask that it be shared. In addition to other factors, the information affirms the honorable personal struggle going on in the student, and the hard struggle of colleges to help these last-stage adolescents engage, stay in gear, get through, and accomplish more growing up.

Readiness to Work

Back to the parental question about their older teenager's readiness to successfully cope with college. For a partial answer, consider *some components of working* that can make a positive difference in adjusting to college or whatever more independent step is taken next. Take them one at a time.

- **Completion:** Does the young person tend to finish what they start, or do they easily get bored or tired and disengage, lacking needed capacity for follow through?
- **Concentration:** Does the young person tend to focus on the task at hand, or do they become easily distracted by more entertaining activity, lacking the needed capacity to pay sustained attention?
- **Consistency:** Does the young person tend to maintain continuity of effort to keep up with significant routine demands, or

do they often let important recurring obligations and needs go unmet?

- **Consequences:** Does the young person tend to learn from the errors of their ways, or do they deny responsibility for the outcomes of their choices and often repeat unwise decisions made?
- **Commitment:** Does the young person tend to keep promises and agreements to self and others, or do they treat these verbal contracts as casually made and easily broken?
- **Cooperation:** Does the young person tend to set some self-interest aside to work with demands from others, or do they insist on doing it their way with no accommodation at all?
- **Control:** Does the young person tend to engage with tasks in a timely way, or do they lack the capacity to delay or deny tempting gratification and escape into a habit of procrastination instead?
- **Communication:** Does the young person tend to level with themselves and others about what is happening, or do they lie to themselves and others to avoid encountering hard realities?

When such behaviors are in evidence, the young person who graduates from parental care at the end of high school is able to say with confidence,

- "I can finish what I begin."
- "I can focus on what needs to be done."
- "I can maintain important continuity of effort."
- "I can learn from the outcomes of my choices."
- "I can keep my promises and agreements."
- "I can give to get along in working with others."
- "I can respond to obligations in a timely way."
- "I can be honest with myself about what's going on."

If you have a college-bound or otherwise departing high school senior who does not have all these work components in functional order, it's best to pay attention. At least let the young person know how these basic skills will be needed to successfully cope with the major transition soon to come. *Functional independence takes a lot of working parts.*

Coping with Problems

Then there is the attitude toward problems in life, which can either make proceeding to more independent functioning easier or more difficult. Think of it this way: *coping with problems can strengthen adolescent growth.*

Problems can be costly and complicating. They take energy to contend with and make life more demanding: "What must I deal with now?" So, consider problems in three common forms: problems as something *to solve*, problems as something *to persevere*, and problems as something *to suffer*.

- Problems to solve can be *confusing*: "I don't know what's going on or what to do in this situation!" Older teenagers find that functional independence comes with a lot more to figure out. These kinds of problems demand to be understood. They prompt the puzzled person to search for a solution or explanation. To cope with problems they need *clarity*.

- Problems to persevere can take *commitment*: "I must keep hanging in there!" The older teenager must develop more self-discipline to support her or his growing independence. These kinds of problems can take constant effort. They prompt the beset person to work through a difficult or tiresome circumstance. To cope with problems they need *persistence*.

- Problems to endure can be *painful*: "Because of what happened I'm really miserable!" Among many losses, older teenagers now find themselves missing the secure comforts of home. These kinds of problems can be unhappy to deal with. They prompt the injured person to feel suffering and sorrow. To cope with problems they need *resilience*.

Of course, major problems are often experienced as some mix of these basic three: "Moving and changing schools in tenth grade upended my life!" Now, after another military move for the reassigned soldier parent, the young person was figuring out the new high school, making every effort to form new relationships, and sorely missing old friends left behind: "I've got problems on top of problems!" Adjustment to college can be equally demanding.

Dealing with Unhappy Problems

In one sense, all unhappy *problems* are self-made because they *are judgment calls* about what is or isn't happening that one decides is not okay. Painful problems are negative comparisons or complaints: "The way things are is *not* how I want them to be!" Now this discrepancy can create dissatisfaction that causes discontent: "I'm feeling really down about how things turned out!" New realities can dash old hopes: "She was great as a friend, but as a roommate in my first apartment, her living habits and late hours are out of line!"

In simplest terms, there are only three ways to alleviate unhappiness problems.

- The person can change how things are to how they want things to be:. "I feel better after getting things to go my way."
- The person can change how they want things to be to fit how things actually are: "I feel better just adjusting to reality."

- The person can do a mix of the two: "I feel better changing what I can and accepting what I can't."

Being Problem-Prone

Deciding they have a problem, a young person tells her- or himself that something needs fixing or changing in their life: "I'm not okay as I am." Or worse, "There's something wrong with me." Now they have created a discrepancy between how things are and how they want things to be, thereby breeding dissatisfaction that can motivate corrective action. They may try to change something about themselves or in their world, or they may create an ongoing sense of discontent with themselves if they cannot: "What's the matter with me?"

So in high school, young people can increasingly wrestle with their physical complaints, as personal appearance has self-esteem and social consequences: "I hate being short and square! I wish I wasn't, but I can't change my basic shape!" And now an unresolved problem puts the young person in a continual internal war, fighting a losing battle, feeling defeated and regretful, or even feeling ashamed on that account, creating a continual source of pain: "I hate how I look!"

Parents might gently explain, "It's best to take responsibility for what you decide to call a problem in your life because problems do not come emotionally cheap. So ask yourself, *Is deciding to have a problem with this part of my life really worth it? Is what I'm dissatisfied about susceptible to change? If so, do I want to invest the personal energy it's going to take to make this change? If not, do I want to keep criticizing myself for how I physically am?* Self-rejection is not a happy way to live."

Confronting a Problem

Young people can sometimes use help choosing their problems wisely: "You may have enough complaints about yourself right now without adding more." Parents might want to explain to their teenager how critical people have a lot of problems to complain about, how grateful people count lots of blessings to be thankful for, and how a very few Zen-like people seem to live mostly untroubled: "Whatever happens is simply how my life is meant to be." People who have peace of mind are relatively problem free.

Having said this, it can take courage to declare, confront, and then address a problem. Judging oneself or one's life as deficient isn't fun. Young people tend to be judgmental about how they are and how their lives are unfolding—what is going right and wrong, well or badly, succeeding or failing, for example. Declaring a problem can address some deficiency and motivate desire for personal change: "I don't have any friends!" However, problems don't just specify something wrong; they can also motivate making something right: "From now on, I'm going to be joiner, not a loner!"

Parents Make Problems

Parents can also add to adolescent problems. "How can you be okay letting schoolwork go?" asks the baffled parent of the capable young teenager who has given up caring about grades because now social life feels more necessary than academic effort. One part of parental oversight can be declaring an adolescent problem where the young person wants his life left alone: "Performance now will affect your future opportunities; therefore, we will supervise your homework to see it gets all done." Conscientious parents are often problem-makers this way, sometimes unpopular on this account: "Quit bugging me!" Reply the parents, "We are on your side, not against you. Keeping after you is a hard part of our job." *Parent as problem-maker is not a popular role.*

When their last-stage adolescent loses financial footing, over-spends, and can't make ends meet, parents should not despair of the young person who is feeling overwhelmed by all the problems more independence brings. At this vulnerable age, corrective parents should never say, "You're nothing but a problem!" Rather, they should keep problems in perspective, explaining how any problem is only a very small part of a very large person, and then proceed to itemize the many things that are going well to recognize many positives that the young person has going for them. And then maybe offer some coaching advice for managing money.

Since the final stage of adolescence is simply a vulnerable time—mastering more adult responsibility—parents who recognize this don't criticize: "Yes, you've gotten behind in your bills and your spending may need correction, but look at all the other ways you're managing independence well."

The Gift of Problems

What to advise your older adolescent about problems? Maybe to treat all problems as *gifts of adversity*—the opportunity to claim hard-earned benefits from coping with obstacles in life.

- Figuring out takes *intelligence*: "Problem-solving is like crack-ing a puzzle or fixing what's wrong. Now I know more than I did before!"
- Coping with challenges takes *perseverance*: "Determination requires not giving up until I achieve what I'm after. Now I've

kept after it!"

- Recovering from hurt takes *resilience*: "Getting over damage is like growing from feeling badly to finding more content. Now I feel better!"

We may not enjoy the problems in our lives, but people often gain capacity from coping with difficulties they bring. Thus, if a young person was engaged with significant hardships growing up, she or he may have claimed valuable strengths resulting from that experience. Increased intelligence, persistence, and resilience can stand them in good stead as normal frustrations and reverses of young adulthood unfold.

What the young person discovers is this: when treated as tests, problems are often opportunities in disguise, having much of lasting value to teach from hard-earned experience. Often, a kind of seasoned confidence can result: "Tough times I've known have prepared me for tough times ahead. I've been there before." To which parents can reply, "And will be again because when all is said and done, problems are not a problem. They are continual challenges that living brings. So treat them respectfully—not as complaints, but as opportunities to master where you can and to adjust where you cannot."

Chapter Eighteen

Emancipation and Demand

● ● ●

"So much is now up to me!"

As one starts to age out of adolescence, personal agency from *societal standing* changes in a lot of powerful ways when officially turning age eighteen. For example, the adolescent now owns their school records, can enlist in the military and get other jobs without parental permission, can enter some business contracts and apply for a loan, has reached the legal age of sexual consent, is eligible for jury duty, can buy some "adult products," with a proven earning record can get a credit card without a parent as co-signer, can vote in local and state and national elections, if they break the law they will be charged as an adult and not a juvenile, can get married (younger in some states), and can get a tattoo and body piercing without parental permission.

This last social empowerment is perhaps why some young people celebrate turning eighteen by getting body-marked: "Why did you do that?" This answer is "because now I can!" They feel more socially emancipated because legally they are. Self-determination grows as societal standing increases: "More is now allowed me than before." So, in some ways, the age of emancipation is empowering. However, it can also be taxing when responsible footing is lost. This is when parents may wonder, "Why can't my college-age child just act grown up?"

Reaching the age of social liberation also can feel daunting: "Now running my life is up to me!" This statement expresses freedom's gift and freedom's burden because the triumph can at times feel overwhelming: "There's so much to take care of!" Thus, there are moments of anxious self-doubt: "I don't know if I can manage it all!"

Many Changes

Most last-stage adolescents have some adult catching up to do. If they want to have independence, solo operation means coping with a lot that needs regular attention. Now life management gets more complicated and demanding in multiple ways.

- They are living apart from home and family shelter.
- They are depending less on parental support.
- They are assuming full self-supervision.
- They are accepting more responsibility.
- They are determining their direction.
- They are budgeting living expenses.
- They are organizing arrangements.
- They are undertaking obligations.
- They are enjoying socializing.
- They are setting priorities.
- They are keeping focus.

- They are looking ahead.
- They are earning money.
- They are paying their bills.

Striving to keep up with all these demands can be extremely challenging. There's so much latitude in their choices, so much to be done, and it all depends on the young person. There's also so much distraction when, looking around, many people of a similar age act mostly out for a good time. Among her cohort of friends, few seem to have a clear direction in life, and when it comes to finding a firm footing in independence, many are slipping and sliding and breaking commitments, to their detriment: broken resolutions, broken plans, broken agreements, broken contracts, broken romantic relationships, broken jobs, broken schooling, broken credit arrangements, broken leases, and even broken laws.

What young people discover, usually at some cost, is that assuming responsible independence is more difficult than they anticipated. In addition, they may have no clear direction in life, no job path into the future they want to follow: "I don't know what I want to do or how to get there!" Anxieties abound in the face of challenges that often feel daunting because they are.

New Complexities

The endgame of the adolescent passage is often the hardest to play both for young person and parents, coming at a bad time since it comes last. Now the older adolescent is likely living away from home for the first time (usually with roommates), at a job, pursuing further education, or both. Although equipped with sufficient will for independence, the young person often does not possess the needed skills. Functional independence proves more demanding than many young people can handle, at least right away.

Just think about the seemingly simple challenge of having a roommate—*the challenge of interdependent living*. Young people especially have to learn to share expenses and joint use of space, protect privacy, cooperate with each other's needs, depend on mutual commitments, distribute responsibilities, tolerate differences, communicate about disagreements, resolve conflicts, and get along with someone whose behaviors one does not always like. All this is only one challenge among many at this more independent age.

During adolescence, life never gets less challenging—only more so. Growing up is always about managing increased complexity. Thus, entering the final stage of adolescence, what I call "trial independence," around the college-age years, a young person has many more demands to attend to with the present and the future both competing for attention. A lot of effort is now required to keep up and to get ahead: "So much is now up to me!" Since effort takes *energy*, begin with that.

The Energy Problem

There's a problem with *personal energy—one's readily available capacity for thinking and action—*that is soon discovered. It is limited. It takes upkeep. And it can, after being spent, momentarily run down or out. Fatigue expresses how sufficient energy is lacking: "I'm tired!" "I need a break!" Managing energy requires judgment about how and when to spend it and when rest and renewal are needed for it to be restored.

Energy is a fundamental life resource, each person's readily available capacity for daily operation. It is easy to take for granted, to behave like it is in infinite supply, is always available, and never runs down or out. However, this is not so. At any moment in time, *personal energy is limited*. Undernourish or overspend it, and human functioning suffers: "I'm worn out!" "I'm done in!" "I'm exhausted!" Enter stress.

Stress

Drained of readily available energy, a person can still deal with overdemand by relying on *an emergency coping response*: resorting to *stress*. Stress has life survival value. It allows the person to force their system to produce an *emergency supply of energy* to override fatigue or cope with crisis, like the procrastinating college student who depends on last-minute deadline motivation to get assignments done: "I stayed up all night to finish my paper on time." However, a physical and emotional price was paid: "I'm really wiped out today!"

No matter how beneficial at the time, relying on stress always depletes the human system. There are questions. Did emergency overdoing justify the cost? Was it worth acting in crisis? Was it worth pushing oneself so hard? Was it worth wearing oneself out? In a life-threatening situation, the answer may be an unqualified yes. However, as a strategy for daily functioning, the answer is often no.

Continual overdoing can be where *lifestyle stress* begins. Depending on stress to cope with unrelenting overdemand, the young person finds that personal costs of excessive effort are typically paid for in at least five psychological and physical ways.

- **Fatigue:** Times when the young person feels worn out, "I just feel tired a lot."
- **Pressure:** Times when the young person feels the strain, "There is more tension to bear."

- **Pain:** Times when the young person feels frequently hurt or troubled, "I have more aches and worries."
- **Burnout:** Times when the young person has a more negative attitude, "I don't always care what happens."
- **Breakdown:** Times when the young person functions less well, "I can't keep up with all I need to remember!"

While often sequential in occurrence, these stress responses can be cumulative so that by the time one gets to breakdown, some fatigue, pressure, pain, and burnout may already be in place. Consider the freshly employed, conscientious young person at their first job with a future, as the long hours and hard striving take a personally expensive toll: "I'm always running behind and running down to get ahead!"

Danger signs for such a beleaguered young person might be longer work hours and less sleep, substance use for socializing and self-care, online diversion at the expense of offline engagement, and neglecting basic nutrition, conditioning, and rest for excitement, entertainment, and escape.

Gatekeepers of Demand

As the older adolescent discovers, independent life is a demanding place to live because there is always much that is necessary and desirable to do. So now the question is: how to moderate stress from ongoing overdemand? Consider three kinds of gatekeeping decisions that can exert necessary self-control: setting attainable goals, merciful standards, and realistic limits.

- **Goals** have to do with *ambition*: how high does she or he want to aspire?

- **Standards** have to do with *excellence*: how well does she or he want to perform?
- **Limits** have to do with *tolerance*: how much can she or he undertake at one time?

A stress-prone young person might be one who feels driven to be the best, aims for perfection, and can't say no to requests or opportunities. Increasingly, to moderate demands, the young person sometimes needs to be able to lower ambition, settle for less than ideal, and to decide that in many cases *some* (not all) is simply going to have to be enough: "I can't always do all I ideally want, and others want of me, and that's okay."

Change and Maintenance

Finally, for the sake of health, a distinction can sometimes be helpful to make at the onset of independent functioning—between the appeal of *change* and the need for *maintenance*.

Change commands attention because it offers what is new and different and more and better. Change is valued because it invigorates, improves, and stimulates human lives. For this reason, change demands are tempting to pursue. This is how you experience excitement and approval and get ahead.

Maintenance demands are less glamorous because all they do is sustain daily functioning—attending to what is ordinary, expected, and routine. For this reason, maintenance demands can be easy to ignore. This is just how you get from one day to the next with the basics taken care of so you don't run down.

You can understand how the college freshman was tempted to sacrifice the needs to study for the test and pay the rent to the desire to attend the party and buy a new outfit. At the end of adolescence,

sometimes it can be easy to pursue change at the expense of maintenance and later have to pick up the stressful cost for this basic self-
neglect: "I should have taken care of business first!"

Parental Advice

What might parents suggest to their struggling last-stage adolescent to keep stress, within reason, from undermining independence?

- Treat occasional stress as expected.
- View ongoing signs of stress with concern.
- Make regular self-maintenance a priority every day.
- Don't pursue tempting changes at the expense of maintenance.
- Set your goals, standards, and limits to avoid constant
  overdemand.
- Try not to make resorting to stress to accomplish daily tasks a
  regular habit.

For the last-stage adolescent, the increased demands of independence create more opportunity for stress. However, if the young person is encouraged to proceed mindfully, she or he can moderate this
demand.

Substance Use

Many young people at this age do not take good care of themselves, as power of want triumphs over power of will, as impulse over-
rules judgment, and as temptation overcomes restraint. They stress
themselves with sleep deprivation, poor dietary habits, task procrastination, credit card indebtedness, nonstop socializing, heavy use
of alcohol and other drugs, and low self-esteem from feeling developmentally incompetent—unable to get their lives together at such
an advanced age. In consequence, some young people in this last

adolescent passage go through periods of despondency, confusion, uncertainty, guilt, shame, worry, and exhaustion. They may resort to substances to cope with demands like with stimulant drugs for studying, sedative drugs to reduce discomfort like from anxiety, or simply recreational drugs to escape their cares like with social relaxants.

The three to five years after high school are a period of increased and varied substance use, interpersonally and personally disorganizing the lives of many young people at a vulnerable age. Unprotected by family, young people at this age are an open market. If your child gets into serious difficulty from poor judgment at this time, always assess the role of substance use in the unhappy events unfolding. If there had been no drinking or other using, would the same choices have been made?

Parental Attitude Matters

For parents who are committed, engaged, settled down, and practical, it is hard to empathize with a child in her or his early twenties who is uncommitted, disengaged, unsettled, and unrealistic. But their impatience, criticism, and anger only make matters worse. Better to express confidence in the older child's capacity to learn from mistakes and to support the will to keep on trying.

Many adolescents in this last stage before young adulthood lose their independent footing and must be encouraged to learn from bad or sad experiences what they did not previously understand. They must learn the hard way by profiting from mistakes and taking responsibility for recovery. Even mature adolescents can lose their footing in trial independence. Trying their hardest, they often didn't do their wisest.

What about the young person who really loses hold and wants to come home to recover? That's very common. In 2011 I wrote about common causes for this return home in my book *Boomerang Kids*. I suggested that parents do not rescue their child from unmet obligations but provide a mutually agreed-upon, time-limited period at home for the child to regroup—to return to rethink and then to reenter the world and struggle with the challenge of trying to claim independence again. Moreover, parents and young adults should contract up front for living-at-home conditions (like giving family help and securing gainful employment) that must be met. Extending this kind of family support is important to do, giving sheltered growing up a little more time. Without it, many bad situations can get worse.

In general, for two to three years after your older adolescent leaves home, it's probably best *not* to repurpose their old bedroom for other household use. That way the young person knows they still have a secure family place to return to should an unexpected need arise.

A major self-esteem drop can occur in trial independence, a painful sense of developmental incompetence. "I'm old enough to be an adult, but I keep messing up!" Tell your child, "Most young people don't find their independent footing without first making some slips because there are so many new responsibilities to learn." Parents can offer counsel as a mature source of life experience that their young person can freely come to for support, understanding, and advice when the going gets tough.

Parents as Mentors

At this last stage of adolescence, parents must change their role from being *managers* (providing supervision and regulation) to becoming *mentors* (providing consultation and advice, when asked).

Barge in and try to control the adolescent's troubled life at this late stage (when a job has been lost and bills are past due), and parents risk rescuing their child from learning life lessons that taking responsibility has to teach—or they potentially cut off communication with a child who refuses to be managed anymore.

By making themselves available as mentors, however, parents offer the benefit of their life experience and ideas if these can be of service as their last-stage adolescent tries to figure out how to choose her way out of the difficulty she has chosen her way into. To effectively discharge this new parenting role, parents must let go of all corrective discipline. They are no longer in the business of judging conduct or making decisions for the young person or bending the conduct of his or her life to their will. Facing real-world consequences will provide discipline enough.

To be an effective mentor means that parents are emotionally approachable. They express faith, not doubt ("You can do it"); patience, not anger ("Keep after it"); consultation, not criticism ("You might try this"); understanding, not disappointment ("It's hard to manage independence"); confidence, not worry ("You have what it takes!"). And they make a positional shift in the relationship. They shift from vertical to horizontal—from being a superior authority to being just a more seasoned peer in the great school life: "I can no longer tell you how to lead your life, but I can offer some understandings about what has worked for me, what didn't, and what I've learned."

As mentors, your role is not dictating what to do or not do. Your role is not to bail your child out of difficulty. Your role is not to express disappointment, criticism, frustration, anger, worry, or despair. Instead, listen empathetically, advise if asked, let go of any responsibility for fixing whatever is going wrong, and offer faith that your young person, having chosen his or her way into trouble, has what it takes to choose his or her way out. You are nonevaluative, noninterfering, respectful, constant, and loving. And if asked, you will share some of your own trials at this time of life, what you learned the hard way, and what lessons you can pass on: "At one point, I thought I didn't have to pay my parking tickets and got myself arrested! That was a hard lesson learned."

As mentors, experienced with your own trial-and-error education in life, let your son or daughter know that independence has always been a struggle, *and the only real failures at this challenging time of life are three: failing to admit the truth, failing to learn from mistakes, and the failure to keep on trying.*

Chapter Ninteen

Emancipation and Opportunity

* * *

"Making my way is partly up to me, and partly not."

Making one's way in the adult world requires mixing exertion with opportunity—depending on one's efforts and engaging with available possibilities. Now one must depend on work habits that have been practiced and put into place. One may also discover that the same educational and occupational chances are not always equally available to all. So consider the importance of self-discipline—work habits—and the power of social favoritism.

Practicing Habits

Practice is the act of intentionally doing some behavior over and over again, a process of repetition that creates habits to strengthen the ease and likelihood that the behavior will be done again. Practice causes conduct to become repetitive, automatic, more patterned, and predictable. People thus become wed to regular schedules, enjoyments, and routines to manage their daily lives. When habits are in place, a sense of familiarity and ease of effort is created.

People depend on habits daily: "I do it this way because I always have." So the last-stage adolescent finds themselves the beneficiary of good habits and the victim of bad habits developed growing up: "I'm pretty good about speaking up for myself, but I can be pretty bad about putting off what I don't want to do." So, taking stock of the habits one has developed growing up, the last-stage adolescent can assert agency and work to strengthen the good and moderate the bad. *Now my job is to manage and develop me.*

Practice Gets Mixed Reviews

Younger adolescents may have been disposed against practice on principle because the experience can oppress individual freedom. Practice can feel like imposing and restrictive work—dull, boring, tiresome, pointless, a waste of personal time, no fun, even painful to repeat: "I get tired of doing this!"

Chores and homework can feel like unrewarding practices and are often resisted on that account. That's also the problem with orders and laws. They command compliance, and adolescents can bridle against such regulation: "Why do I have to?" *Rules require repetition.*

Yet these same young opponents of unwanted practice can embrace it when it has personal value—in recreational, athletic, and social activities, for example: "I can play this game forever!" "I love working out." "I just like hanging out with my friends!" *Pleasure promotes repetition.*

Practice is a very tricky issue for parents to manage with their adolescent because while it can be empowering in many ways, it can be disabling in others. To the good, it can be an investment in wellness; to the bad, it can be a seduction into self-harm.

Consider how this contradiction might be so.

Practice Is Habit-Forming

Practice is powerful because it is habit-forming, and people are creatures and captives of habits. To the positive are helpful disciplines and routines to be relied upon; to the problematic are harmful cravings and compulsions to which one can fall prey.

Positive habits can seem harder to start and easier to stop (like practicing moderation), while negative habits often seem easier to start and harder to stop (like indulging in excess).

With good and bad habits, repetitive practice has created a stubborn pattern of behavior on which one has come to rely.

So, talk to your adolescent about the power of habits. Start by explaining how human habits can be complicated and contradictory. For example,

- Good habits can help; bad habits can hinder.
- Good habits are rewarding; bad habits are tempting.
- Good habits build confidence; bad habits hurt esteem.
- Good habits can keep us well; bad habits can do us harm.
- Good habits can be hard to start; bad habits can be hard to stop.
- Good habits can create discipline; bad habits can create dependency.
- Good habits can be hard to keep up; bad habits can be easy to fall into.

To the good and bad, as mentioned, people are both creatures and captives of habits that dictate much human conduct. I believe part of the parental job is to help their teenager understand the influential power of habits. In addition, by example, instruction, and encouragement they can help the teenager develop a set of self-management habits that can serve her or him well after leaving home and undertaking the challenges of independent living: "From my parents saving some money each month, I learned to do the same."

Habits Take Practice

Building work habits that support self-discipline takes practicing repeated efforts over time. Such effort often is not fun to do. At an age when new and different and novel and exciting activities command interest, recurring familiar exercises—like nightly homework, for example—can feel like a waste of valuable time: "I hate practice! It's doing the same thing over and over! It's boring! It's not fun! Why would anyone want to practice?"

Parents need to have a positive answer to this question because practicing turns out to be very valuable when it builds significant life skills. For example,

> **Enabling expression** to be understood: "I can speak up about what I want."
>
> **Building routines** to rely on: "I can schedule and organize my work."
>
> **Focusing attention** on an activity: "I can concentrate on what needs doing."
>
> **Training capacity** to master a skill: "I can learn to perform this well."

Changing behavior to self-correct: "I can do now, and stop delaying for later."

Meeting commitments to rely on: "I can keep promises to myself and others."

Strengthening willpower to motivate effort: "I can make myself work hard."

Becoming good at practicing can benefit a teenager in many ways that support growth of *self-discipline,* that set of reliable work habits that build competence and confidence. While it does require effort, practice is not repellent. It can be truly empowering, supporting development of many capacities that parents want their teenager to develop and that the young person is glad to be able to count on. *Many young people who enjoy playing competitive sports learn to appreciate how practice improves athletic performance and can even feel enjoyable to do.*

Managing Bad Habits

Then there is the downside when practicing self-defeating behavior leads to self-harm: "I started vaping to fit in at high school; now I'm coughing, my breathing is harder, but it's really tough to give it up." So maybe, with a couple of friends who have developed the same concern, they form a "quitting club" to help each other change their harmful habit: "Wanting to reach for a hit, we can call each other instead."

Trying to curb a bad habit, however, and wanting to quit are often not enough, because with repetition, the habit has become perversely relied upon: "Doing bad can feel so good!" Thus, in the self-harming extreme, a teenager feels like cutting herself again, or binging and purging again, or getting drunk or high again. In such cases, simple determination to stop may not be a sufficient deterrent: "I can't make myself stop!"

Practices of the self-destructive kind can breed a very strong temptation to continue. Thus, the self-harming young person needs to have an alternative plan in place to follow when the urge to repeat the negative behavior arises. Such a plan might include asking, "What can I do instead? Who can I talk to? Where can I go for support?" This is part of what support groups, therapy, or inpatient or outpatient treatment help to install—planning a new self-management practice to call on when old repetition threatens so that positive behavior change, recovery, has a chance to take hold.

For example, after four years of hard college partying, a young man has developed a well-practiced social habit of excessive drinking he intended to moderate after graduation. But it wasn't that easy. Now out in the world, he kept trying to cut back to get on with his life, but a little always led to a lot—and a lot to too much, and he was back acting like he no longer wanted. He couldn't get himself to stop. He had practiced himself into a habit of dependency. That's when he got himself some quitting help. Through a friend, he ended up in a support group of people who understood what he was up against, offering help one day at a time. So now, to withstand the urge to drink and to lead a sober life instead, he attended an assisted abstinence program, Alcoholics Anonymous, where sober living is supported. Instead of giving in to the old drinking habit, he had alternative choices to practice: maybe he could read in the *Big Book,* work the twelve steps, call his sponsor, or go to a meeting rather than reach for the bottle: "Now when I feel like drinking, I have a positive alternative I didn't have before."

How do you break free of a self-defeating pattern? Often, you do so not by directly resisting and stopping it. Instead, with vigilance you are alert to the old temptation when it arises and commit to practice a positive alternative instead.

Practicing Beneficial Change

Then there is practice as approximation or pretense—you "act" how you would like to become. To some degree, we are creatures of our own creation. The more often we act a certain way, the more that way becomes familiar and easier to do again.

- You can become more honest by practicing truth-telling.
- You can become more independent by practicing responsibility.
- You can become more communicative by practicing speaking up.
- You can become more trustworthy by practicing meeting commitments.
- You can become more solvent by practicing saving instead of spending.
- You can become more organized by practicing order and relying on routines.

With practice, people learn to shape and reshape themselves all the time. Practice can be a formative act. The last-stage adolescent needs to understand "with practice, I can change how I live within myself, with other people, and in the world." Practicing independence is empowering when it helps instill more grown-up skills to take care of themselves in an adult way: "Now I can hold my job, pay my bills, and take care of myself."

Thus, parental advice to their teenager might be "Keep repeating your good habits because they keep you functioning well. And should you ever become trapped in practicing a bad habit you feel unable to change, that is a good time to find help to get yourself out."

There may be another hard reality to discuss: *self-discipline* may not be enough to advance yourself because the possibility of *social favoritism* can obstruct making your way or even do you harm.

Social Favoritism

Social favoritism is preferential treatment that unfairly gives more positive value, assistance, and opportunity to those in majority power who possess some favored characteristic and denies equal value, assistance, and opportunity to those in the contrasting minority who do not. It puts one group up by keeping another group down and is socially oppressive in this way.

Majority and minority can be affected by this inequity, and abiding lessons can be learned on both sides. For example, the majority might come to believe they are better than others—entitled to preferential treatment and superior standing—while the minority might come to believe they are not as good as others, resigned to subordinate treatment and inferior standing. Such favoritism can be formative because social freedom and self-definition are at stake.

To begin a discussion, a mom might explain about one common form of social favoritism, *sexism*: "When my grandmother was your age, the most common jobs a girl could usually aspire to were the feminine five: factory, service, secretarial, teaching, or nursing. Any occasional exception only illustrated the prevalence of this rule. Since then, more opportunity and advancement have opened up for women, but the occupational playing field has still not leveled out. A kind of partiality can still be in play that takes many forms. In my grandmother's case, men were allowed more occupational mobility than women, just as whites were allowed more occupational mobility than nonwhites, and richer people had more occupational opportunities than poorer. However, through the efforts of others, today you have more freedom of choice than two generations ago."

Yet, the more conditions change, the more one notices when they stay the same. Consider this complaint: "It's so unfair! They get physical conditioning opportunity that we don't!" The high school junior was complaining how the single weight room had been taken over by male athletes, the jocks ("jerks," she called them), who created a hostile place for female athletes like her who wanted to strength train too. They were made to feel unwelcome there: "Who wants to work out where you're being made fun of?"

Thus the young woman came to this unhappy conclusion: "In high school athletics, guys get taken more seriously here, their sports are more highly valued, and they are better supported than girls."

What's going on? The answer can be a variation of *social favoritism*, in this case providing preferential treatment to males over females.

Many are the "isms" that can advantage some majority and disadvantage some minority where there is a contrasting we/they difference between them. As an example, with sexism, where social favoritism is based on a binary view of sexual gender, male is favored, female is disfavored.

In this case, your teenage daughter's growing freedom can be unfairly limited because she is a girl. So parents are well advised to pay attention to the social treatment their growing daughter receives. Not only can she be placed at an unfair disadvantage, she can also be endangered.

How might parents want to respond to their teenage daughter should this unhappy form of social favoritism come her way? To empower, support, and protect her as best they can, it's important to understand four basic ways that social favoritism, in this case sexism, can harm.

How Social Favoritism Harms

Prejudice can lower self-worth: "Women are not as capable and important as men." Feeling put down by this comparison, at worst your daughter can believe she is inadequate and inferior, "less than," just for being female. *The power of prejudice can be the poison of self-rejection.*

Discrimination can obstruct mobility: "Men are better suited for this kind of work than women." Denied an equal chance, at worst your daughter can have to accept reduced choices for advancement. *The power of discrimination can be the limitation of opportunity.*

Harassment can create a loss of personal safety: "If they know what's good for them, women better do what men say." At worst, exposed to male threats and acts of violence, your daughter can feel endangered. *The power of harassment can be the exploitation of fear.*

Complicity can reduce social oversight: "People who know about what's happening just look the other way." At worst, when sexual inequity and injury are ignored, your daughter can feel not publicly supported. *The power of complicity can be silent consent to wrongdoing.*

What Parents Might Say

So, should any of these sexist mistreatments come their daughter's way, what might parents say?

- **About prejudice:** "That kind of attitude and expression communicates nothing wrong about you but exposes the ignorance or ill-will of the speaker."

- **About discrimination:** "To be rejected or excluded because you are a woman violates your equal rights, and you can make that case if you so choose."
- **About harassment:** "To be sexually threatened or harmed is a time to get help and take what steps you can to stop the mistreatment and perpetrator."
- **About complicity:** "Should any of these mistreatments happen to you, and those who know act like they don't, this is a time to demand their attention."

Most important, should your adolescent fall prey to any of the four forms of social favoritism—be it based on sex, sexuality, race, disability, nationality, culture, religion, primary language, economic background, or any other characteristic—let the young person know that you want to be told in order to support the adolescent during a hurtful time: "You are not alone. It can be scary to speak up and stand up for yourself, and we want to help in any way we can."

Addressing Favoritism

Finally, to the parent who disbelieves in social favoritism in general, or in sexism in particular, despite what her or his daughter reports, ask that mother or father to simply look at the data. For example, "How come, after over two hundred years, the United States has never had the benefit of a female president?" To young women like their daughter, the social favoritism message has been clear: "If you're female, you can't aspire to fill the highest public office in this land."

I believe it's wise for parents to respect any reports from their growing teenager (daughter or son) of prejudice, discrimination, harassment, or complicity that puts the young person down, keeps them out, threatens their well-being, or when such mistreatment is publicly known but socially ignored. Why listen to them?

Because when it comes to sexism, racism, colorism, lingualism, functionalism, nationalism, classism, or any other form of social favoritism that advantages similarity to the dominant majority and penalizes the minority for being different, such inequitable treatment of their adolescent can be demeaning, unfairly limiting, endangering, and isolating and thus can do a lot of harm. Parents can beneficially share any experience of social favoritism that adversely affected them—maybe still does—and how they dealt and deal with this mistreatment: "My folks told me how they've had to deal with social unfairness so that I can benefit from what they've learned."

Chapter Twenty

Emancipation and Expectations

● ● ●

"What will my future bring?"

"Living at home, my parents decided how my life was supposed to go, but now taking charge is up to me." When the challenge of this governing handoff is unappreciated, the helping power of expectations may not be fully understood. Emancipation creates the adolescent freedom and responsibility to set working expectations for one's life. So, back to a topic earlier discussed.

Expectations Matter

The expectations one creates can have a lot of bearing on how smoothly or harshly this transition to functional independence unfolds. Managing so much more freedom takes a lot of getting used to. Having realistic expectations can be helpful in making this adjustment, while unrealistic expectations can make it harder to bear.

Thus, consider what expectations are, their powerful positive functions, how costly unrealistic and unmet expectations can be, and what advice parents might helpfully give.

Expectations are ideas that have proactive and adaptive value. They are chosen mental sets that help people estimate the experience to come, maintain valued continuity one day to the next, and help people adjust to change. Much that we did today we did yesterday and shall do again tomorrow, yet every day brings new and different circumstances and challenges. So on one hand we need to count on repeating the expected to create continuity, and on the other we need to be ready to adjust our thinking to fit unexpected changes.

Change Changes Expectations

Changing circumstances and conditions usually cause people to adjust their expectations to accept a new reality. For example, consider several common adjustments parents have to make when their child grows into adolescence.

- Now the parents who were told much by the open and disclosing child are often told less by the teenager who wants more freedom of privacy. Expect to be less fully informed.
- Now the parents who were the child's favored playmates are often supplanted by the teenager's preference for companionship with peers. Expect that family will compete with friends.
- Now the willing and cooperative child can frequently become actively and passively resistant, with more arguing and delay with their requests. Expect more opposition to assistance and compliance.

No love is lost, but parents do need to adjust their expectations to living with a more individually and independently growing, more self- and socially preoccupied adolescent. So gradually and sometimes grudgingly, they change their expectations to fit the shifting reality that adolescent growth has created: "We know she'll keep more to herself, needs more time with friends, and will have more disagreements with us." They change old expectations to accept a new reality as their adolescent grows so they can more smoothly get along.

This said, while parents hold on to some old expectations, like how respectful communication still needs to be conducted within the family, they let go of those that have clearly become outgrown. So from their own personal experience, parents know how important changing expectations to fit an altered reality can be. To a comparable degree, the end of adolescence demands a major adjustment of self-expectations to engage with the challenge of functional independence. Part of getting one's independent house in order is furnishing it with realistic expectations.

In general, expectations deal with what's happening in the following four powerful ways: with predictions, ambitions, conditions, and limitations. Each kind of expectation has affirming impact when fulfilled, and unhappy emotional consequences when not. *Expectations are mental sets that can have powerful emotional consequences when met and not met.*

- **Predictions** are about expecting what *will* happen—thinking ahead, considering possibilities, forecasting problems, and calculating risks. *Predictions have the power to anticipate:* "I thought this might happen, so I was ready when it did." Predictions prepare for what happens next. Unmet and unrealistic predictions can cause *worry* and *anxiety* from ignorance: "What's going to happen now?"

- **Ambitions** are about expecting what one *wants* to happen—creating plans, setting goals, satisfying purposes, pursuing dreams. *Ambitions have the power to motivate:* "I go after what matters to me." Ambitions focus on advancement and fulfillment. Unmet and unrealistic ambitions can cause *sadness* and *disappointment* from feeling let down: "I didn't get what I worked and hoped for."
- **Conditions** are about expecting what *should* happen—following rules, keeping promises, meeting plans, performing up to standards. *Conditions have the power to obligate.* Unmet and unrealistic obligations can cause *anger* and *guilt* when a commitment is unmet:. "I really let myself down!"
- **Limitations** are expectations that *set* how much doing a person *can* tolerate happening. *Limitations have the power to regulate*: "I can refuse and say no to myself and others." Unmet and unrealistic limits can allow excessive demand, creating *stress*: "I overcommitted and feel overwhelmed doing so much!"

To the good, in all four ways, expectations help people live one day to the next with some degree of confidence, clarity, and comfort. To the bad, unrealistic expectations can lead to a lot of emotional distress when predictions are unlikely, ambitions are extreme, conditions are unreachable, or limitations are insufficient.

Violated positive expectations can have painful emotional consequences, including anxiety, disappointment, guilt, and stress. So when something happens or doesn't happen that you—or your teenager—feels upset about, it's always worth asking, *What was I expecting?* Sometimes normalizing hard experience with adjusted expectations can make the unwanted easier to accept: "I found out the hard way that less class attendance can lower my grade." Or, consider a common romantic letdown: "I was hoping 'in love' meant that we'd never seriously disagree. Now I know better. Disagreement isn't something wrong to get upset about. It comes with getting serious with each other. It's to be expected. As we get to know each other better, we'll keep discovering more differences between us." Thus realistic expectations can lessen emotional upset.

Parental Advice

What to advise your departing adolescent about handling these complicated and essential mental sets? Parents might suggest the following:

- "Create predictions: keep thinking ahead, knowing you cannot foresee everything."
- "Create ambitions: keep pursuing your goals, knowing you cannot reach them all."
- "Create conditions: keep striving to do your best, knowing you cannot be perfect."
- "Create limitations: keep doing what you can, knowing that some is often enough."

The art of setting and resetting realistic expectations is a challenge at every age. I'm reminded of President Abraham Lincoln's observation: "I believe most folks are as happy as they make up their minds to be." I think choosing what expectations to hold is one important way people can happily or unhappily "make up their minds."

Perhaps the most important adolescent expectation for parents to encourage is *hope*.

Adolescent Hope

Never say you "give up" on your last-stage adolescent as the latest misjudgment or loss of footing occurs: "My parents say I'm hopeless!"

No. Parents need to be hope holders to the last, always believing in positive possibilities.

When an adolescent displays signs of losing hope, parents need to show that it can be recovered. For example, consider how parents responded to their emotionally devastated teenager: "After his girlfriend broke up the relationship—she was his first love—our son seemed inconsolable. Overwhelmed by sadness, he felt he had lost all that mattered to him, and for a while it seemed like he was losing his will to carry on. So while we gave him our emotional support, we also reconnected him to good things in his life, particularly those that lay ahead, to look forward to. We wanted to keep him company in his sadness, but we also wanted to give grounds for hope. After all, the strength he had to commit his caring this time will be there for him when he falls in love again. We didn't want him to give up on himself, succumb to despondency, and maybe choose to do himself harm."

Their concern of dire consequences from despair, or utter loss of hope, is not unfounded. On September 7, 2019, the *New York Times* reported, "Across the country, suicide has been on the rise. In October, the Centers for Disease Control and Prevention reported that suicide had become the second leading cause of death for people age 10 to 23." This is roughly the life span of adolescence as I understand it.

When it comes to leading one's own life, helping your adolescent keep her or his hopes up is truly important. Setting positive expectations is how to do so: "I will find what works for me." "I want to do want matters to me." "I should be content with some as enough."

Sharing Personal History

While the young adolescent may seem to discount any worldly knowledge parents have acquired from longer life experience, the departing adolescent becomes more inclined to seek and accept the knowledge parents possess. For example, the notion of independence and working for self-support has raised questions about how and where the young person will find work. In most cases, schooling so far has provided little preparation on this score. There has been very little occupational or career education. Parents can make up for some of this loss by describing some of their job history. None of this is to take charge of the young person's life, only to share what may be worth practically knowing from one generation to the next.

A parent can say, "You've mostly known me in the job I have now. But I've had many jobs since high school, one somehow following to the next, and I want to tell you what my path has been so you can be persistent and patient with your own." Then the parent can share their sequence of jobs to where they are currently employed. They can tell how one job happened to lead to another. They can describe the play of choice, plan, and happenstance in how they made their occupational way: "I want to share this not to tell you how to proceed, but to show you how many jobs it's common to have making one's way through the world of work. A career path can be pretty unexpected, but for good and ill, each job had something to teach."

Parents share this so the newly independent child can appreciate their meandering journey through the world of work, the ups and downs by intent and accident that marked their occupational history. What challenges have parents faced, and what lessons have they learned? How did they lose their way to find their way? What did each job experience provide?

Having this talk can be appreciated: "It turns out that my parents didn't start out knowing what their current job would be. They had to try and discover their way through many different jobs to where they are now. I guess that may also go for me. I'm going to have to find out what work I will end up doing."

Then there is the final parental challenge of dealing with increasing adult differences as their adolescent continues to grow into a more individual and independent person when social life and partnership experience exercise a changing influence on how that grown daughter or son now self-defines.

Accepting Adult Differences

By example and instruction, parents often have fundamental beliefs and practices that they assume their grown child will continue—be these ethically, culturally, religiously, sexually, politically, or lifestyle based: "We expect our kids to keep and carry on all our family values." Yes, they partly will, and no, they partly won't.

When this heritage is repudiated by older offspring, parents can feel a significant loss of continuity: "We assumed we'd always share the same values and beliefs!" Explains the young person, "Thinking and acting exactly like you is not how I am anymore." In unhappy surprise, parents wonder, "How did our young adult turn out this way?" This is not what they valued, modeled, or taught. At worst, disappointment, betrayal, or even estrangement can follow: "Our grown child's change of mind has cut us off!" Consider one variation of this outcome.

Politically, for example, parents can feel like what they devotedly followed has been rejected: "How can such liberal parents end up with such a conservative son?" "How can such conservative parents end up with such a liberal daughter?" In deeply partisan times, how can parents of one passionate political view come to terms with an older adolescent or young adult who is firmly wed to its opposite political persuasion?

Start by considering the changing developmental influence of parents as their child grows.

Similarity to Parents at the Beginning

Childhood, up to about ages eight or nine, is a time for identifying with parents and imitating them to build a close attachment with them. The child does so to create a primary adult relationship on which the girl or boy can securely depend and that at this age leads to admiration: "I want to be just like Mom and Dad!"

So, to the extent the little girl or boy has any political preference, they loyally mirror parental beliefs. For example, in an election year, for decoration's sake, they might show off national campaign buttons to friends: "I vote how my parents do!"

Childhood is the age of growing commonality with parents, identifying with their ways. Adolescence, beginning around ages nine to thirteen and ending around eighteen to twenty-three, is propelled by two developmental drives—for divergence and for separation. Now the parental challenge is to stay caringly and communicatively connected with their changing daughter or son while adolescence increasingly grows them apart, which it is meant to do.

- **Differentiating** from childhood and parents, the teenager experiments with more individual expression, ultimately creating a uniquely fitting identity: "I am my own person."
- **Detaching** from childhood and parents, the teenager asserts more freedom of choice, ultimately assuming a functional independence: "I make my own decisions."

Adolescence is the age of growing contrast to parents.

A challenge for parents is to not take these changes personally. Although adolescent rebellion, for example, can be acted out against them, it is not primarily about them. Rather, it expresses the young person striving for liberation from the old definition of them as a child. For the sake of individuality and independence, the young person is using contrast to parents to help make this growing transformation occur.

Adolescence normally creates more diversity and independence from parents, which can sometimes be expressed in adopting opposing beliefs; college-age youth, caught up in student activism, may even convert to another political affiliation. For those parents whose politics are anchored in strong partisan conviction and commitment, this contrast can be hard to tolerate. So what might these hard-pressed parents do?

The focal question might be how much difference do parents want to make of this political difference? At this juncture, beware political arguments that breed hard feelings because they rarely yield resolution. Each party becomes more wed to their beliefs by defending and criticizing back, often intensifying the division between them.

What might they want to consider instead?

- Rather than treat a political difference as a barrier to getting along and listening with their mind made up, treat it as a bridge, a talking opportunity to better understand each other.
- Rather than take personal offense, respect the individuality and independence of their grown child's political convictions and the bravery to assert their self in this contrasting way.
- Rather than treat political differences as primary, keep them in perspective as only a small part of a larger person, and appreciate the loving history and abiding commonalities they still share.

Sometimes political and other belief differences between parent and adult child can rend the relationship, sacrificed on the altar of partisan disagreement: "If we can't agree politically, we'll never get along!"

So back to the earlier question: how much difference do parents want this political difference to make? Do they want to give it the power to divide, divorce, or disown? By doing so, not only do parents sustain a grievous loss, but they inflict a grievous injury to their rejected child—the severing of family ties.

Throughout the course of their adult child's journey, growing diversity between parents and offspring will continue to unfold. Thus the parent's constant task is to keep adjusting their expectations to fit their older daughter's or son's ever-changing life. This is why *the end of adolescence brings the greatest parenting challenge of all: to hold on with loving commitment, while at the same time giving the greater loving, which is to let the loved one go.*

Epilogue

● ● ●

The Fifth Freedom: Reconciliation

Letting go the bad and holding on to the good

There is no perfect child or parent. There is no perfect childhood or adolescence. There are only parent and teenager relating the best they can, gradually becoming increasingly independent of, and different from, each other as they grow apart. In the course of this necessary separation and redefinition, an abrasive process, misunderstandings and mistakes will occasionally cause one or both parties to end up feeling injured or offended: "That really hurt!"

Mostly these offenses are of minor and passing impact: "When you came home late from work, you could be really impatient to live with." "When you got busy with friends, it could be really hard to get your attention." There were lots of normal trials of day-to-day getting along. No big deal. With acceptance of each other's imperfections, such irritations and offenses were readily let go.

However, in some cases there can be harder stuff that happened. Short of ongoing abuse, I mean situations where there were some impulsive words or damaging actions that the parent or adolescent wishes they could take back or could have done differently. These are occasions where the painful past is unhappily present between them and can still arouse hard feelings when remembered: "I wish you hadn't stolen money from us and made everyone in the family feel so unsafe!" "I wish you hadn't divorced and broken up the family!" There can be lingering regret and remorse on both sides: "I wish our life together had played out differently!"

For the departing adolescent and the deserted parent, it can be hard to grow forward with each other when one is still sorely tied to the past. What to do? They might be able to free themselves from the hold of former suffering by engaging in a process of *reconciliation*. This requires letting go of old unhappiness with *forgiveness* of self and of the other (of guilt and resentment) and holding on to the value of their own and each other's past and ongoing contributions to the relationship (of gratitude and support) with *appreciation*.

Over the years when I was still in private practice, I would occasionally do *reconciliation counseling* for a strained parent–adult child relationship. The goal was to help the *aggrieved* parties get unstuck from pain and start to build a working foundation for moving on. To this end, I tried to help them understand the difference between talking about *grievance* and talking about *grief* over whatever had unhappily happened.

I suggested that when talking about grievance at offense and feeling wronged, it is easy to focus on resentment and to cast blame, often encouraging the other person to make a defensive response: "Well, what about all the harm you did to me?"

When talking about grief from pain about what happened and feeling hurt, however, it is possible to focus on injury, perhaps encouraging the other person to make an empathetic response: "I didn't know how damaging for you this was."

This is the difference between making a critical or a compassionate response, one that shuts communication down or one that opens it up. The goals of reconciliation discussions between parent and departing adolescent or young adult, who are stuck in a hard emotional place with each other because of lingering unhappiness, were

- To encourage empathetic understanding between them.
- To give grief a full hearing for unhappiness to be expressed.
- To honor the hard side of their relationship by hearing painful history.
- To now focus on the positive contributions they have made to each other.
- To talk about how they wish their relationship would more happily carry on.

Between parent and grown child, when past hurts stand in the way of the future relationship, then an attempt at reconciliation and the final freedom it can give may be worthwhile to try.

About the Author

• • •

Retired after over thirty years in private counseling practice in Austin, Texas, psychologist Carl Pickhardt continues to write books about parenting adolescents and in his popular blog for *Psychology Today*, "Surviving (Your Child's) Adolescence," which has received over twelve million reads.

He received his BA in English from Harvard in 1961, his MEd in counseling from the Harvard Graduate School of Education in 1966, and his PhD in counseling psychology from the University of Texas in 1970. He is a member of the American Psychological Association.

In addition to past magazine, newspaper, and internet columns, he has written extensively about the psychology of growing up in nonfiction (sixteen previous parenting books) and in fiction (three young adult novels: *The Trout King*, *The Art Lover*, and *The Helper's Apprentice*), as well as eight books of illustrated psychology, starting with *From Cell to Society* (Houghton Mifflin, 1965).

Holding On While Letting Go is his latest nonfiction book about the parent/adolescent relationship and the coming-of-age passage.

More information about Carl Pickhardt and his various books may be found on his website:

www.carlpickhardt.com

Other Parenting Books by the Author

● ● ●

"Who Stole My Child?": Parenting Through Four Stages of Adolescence (Central Recovery Press, 2018).

Surviving Your Child's Adolescence: How to Understand, and Even Enjoy, the Rocky Road to Independence (Jossey-Bass/Wiley, 2013).

Boomerang Kids: Why So Many of Our Kids Are Failing on Their Own and How Parents Can Help (Sourcebooks, 2011).

Why Good Kids Act Cruel: The Hidden Truth About the Pre-Teen Years (Sourcebooks, 2010).

Keys to Successful Stepfathering, 2nd edition (Barron's Educational Series, 2010).

Stop the Screaming: How to Turn Angry Conflict with Your Child into Positive Communication (Palgrave Macmillan, 2009).

The Future of Your Only Child: How to Guide Your Child to a Happy and Successful Life (Palgrave Macmillan, 2008).

The Connected Father: Understanding Your Unique Role and Responsibilities During Your Child's Adolescence (Palgrave Macmillan, 2007).

The Everything Parent's Guide to Children and Divorce* (Adams Media, 2006).

The Everything Parent's Guide to the Strong-Willed Child* (Adams Media, 2005).

The Everything Parent's Guide to Positive Discipline* (Adams Media, 2005).

Keys to Developing Your Child's Self-Esteem (Barron's Educational Series, 2000).

Keys to Raising a Drug-Free Child (Barron's Educational Series, 1999).

Keys to Parenting the Only Child (Barron's Educational Series, 1997).

The Case of the Scary Divorce: A Jackson Skye Mystery (Magination Press, American Psychological Association, 1997).

Keys to Single Parenting (Barron's Educational Series, 1996).